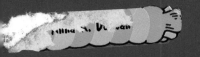

Shakespeare's Stories

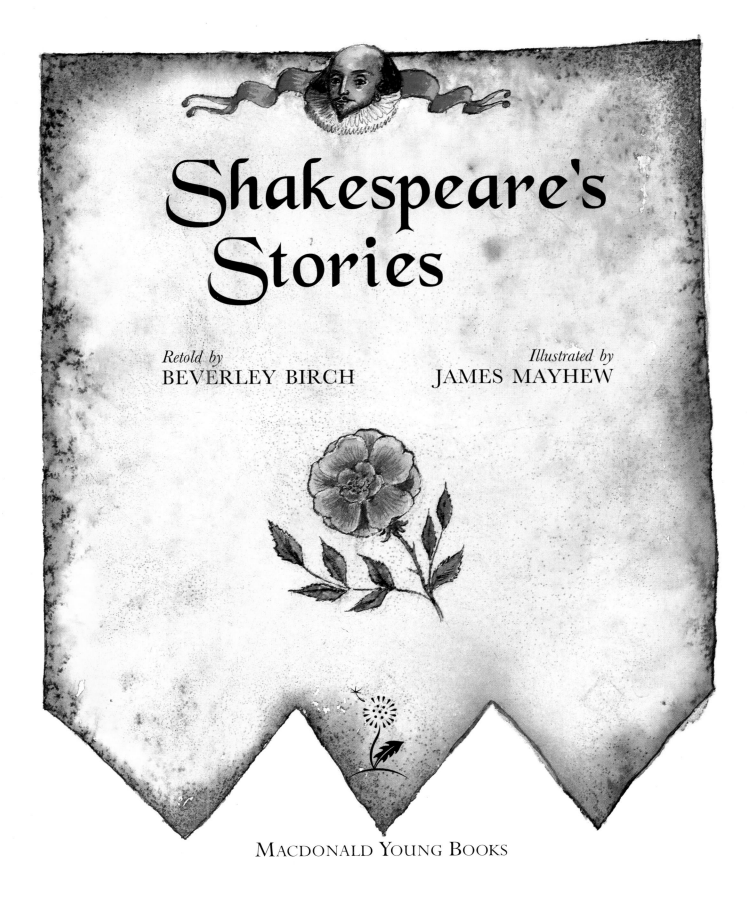

Shakespeare's Stories

Retold by
BEVERLEY BIRCH

Illustrated by
JAMES MAYHEW

MACDONALD YOUNG BOOKS

For Marion Meaden — B.B.
For my mother and father, with love — J.M.

Text copyright © 1988 Beverley Birch
Illustrations copyright © 1997 James Mayhew

First published in 1988 by
Macdonald & Co (Publishers) Limited

This edition first published in 1997 by
Macdonald Young Books
an imprint of Wayland Publishers Ltd
61 Western Road
Hove
East Sussex
BN3 1JD

Reprinted in paperback in 1998

Printed and bound in Portugal by Edições ASA.
Designed by Dalia Hartman and James Mayhew

British Library Cataloguing in Publication Data available.

ISBN: 0 7500 2672 3

Contents

Romeo & Juliet

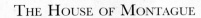

THE HOUSE OF MONTAGUE

Old Montague

Lady Montague

Romeo
their son

Benvolio
Romeo's friend

Friar Lawrence
*friend and adviser to
Romeo*

THE HOUSE OF CAPULET

Old Capulet

Lady Capulet

Juliet
their daughter

Nurse
*friend and adviser to
Juliet*

Tybalt
Juliet's cousin

The Prince of
Verona

Paris
a relative of the prince

Mercutio
*a relative of the prince
and Romeo's friend*

Within the ancient walls of fair Verona lived two families, the Capulets and the Montagues. Both, alike, were rich and honoured in the city, but both alike were poisoned by a hatred that festered deep within them. Its cause was lost long in the distant past. Only the vicious anger lingered, like the rotten odour of a crime, polluting both the families.

Capulets hated Montagues, and Montagues hated Capulets: each son and daughter, cousin, uncle, aunt, each servant, cat and dog had bred the venom deep into their veins. Twice already in the blistering heat of this high summer their quarrel boiled to vicious brawls across the narrow streets and sleepy squares. Now it flared again: two bored servants of the house of Capulet taunted two servants of the Montagues, and in a flash the swords and daggers sliced amid the snarlings of wild men, like savage animals.

A young Montague named Benvolio rushed to part the struggling men; Tybalt, a young Capulet who burned for every chance to vent his fury on a Montague, leapt out into the fray. Within minutes the street was filled with Montague fighting Capulet, while women of the city hurried children in behind closed doors and pulled the shutters down against the chopping swords. And once again Verona's citizens drew rusty weapons from retirement and ran out to part the foes who seemed to have no other aim in life except to butcher one another.

There was one of the house of Montague who did not flourish a sword that day. Young Romeo was far from that blighted scene, plunged in a moody solitude. Benvolio, still panting from his efforts as a peace-maker at the brawl, met brooding Romeo wandering across the square and joined him, anxious to discover why his cousin shunned all company.

It was not difficult to tap the cause of Romeo's ache: he longed to tell. He pined for love! A lady, Rosaline by name, bewitched him with her beauty, but would not return his love . . .

Benvolio was quick with good advice. 'Be ruled by me,' he urged his cousin Romeo. 'Forget to think of her! Examine other beauties.'

Romeo would have none of this. He wanted to remain locked in his love-sick melancholy. Forget Rosaline? He could never forget the precious treasure of her beauty!

In the great ballroom of his house old Capulet stood smiling a genial welcome to his guests, urging them to drink and feast and the musicians to strike up a merry note for all to dance. He offered a cordial hand to the company of maskers who came to grace his ball, and Mercutio and Benvolio were swept away on the wings of gaiety. Amid the twinkling lights and gleaming floors, soft-slippered feet pranced and danced to the swish of silks and velvets. But Romeo saw nothing of this scene. He had seen a vision he had never seen before, a girl of such exquisite beauty. . .

He had seen Juliet. Across the dancing room her glow had caught him in its light and put all thought of Rosaline to instant flight. Juliet seemed to burn with such radiance that all else receded into glowing dark: Romeo saw nothing but her gleaming hair and shining eyes . . .

In rapt wonder he stood watching her. Dare he move closer?

Tybalt saw the young masker watch his cousin Juliet as though his eyes would never drink enough, and he became suspicious. He drew near, heard Romeo's voice enquiring of a passing servant who the stranger was, and anger shot through him with age-old viciousness.

'This by his voice should be a Montague,' he breathed. 'Fetch me a sword!' he told a servant. How dare a Montague invade a Capulet house, disguised, and sneer at their revelling!

Old Capulet saw his fiery nephew arming for some fight and hurried forward. Not at this feast! Not in this house!

'I'll not endure him,' hissed Tybalt, throwing off his uncle's hand.

'He shall be endured! *I* say he shall!' thundered Capulet. 'Am I master here, or you? You'll make a mutiny among my guests! You are an insolent youth. Be quiet, or I'll make you quiet.'

Flaming with thwarted hate, Tybalt withdrew. But he had not given up. He would still find his time to challenge this Montague who thumbed his nose at them!

Blind to the struggle being waged so near at hand, Romeo had drawn close to Juliet. Across the bobbing heads of dancers Juliet had seen the mysterious young man who seemed to glide towards her as if some witchcraft beyond his power propelled him on. The wonderment that shone even from his hidden face, touched an answering, slumbering flame in her. She looked, and she was captured.

She waited for him, enthralled. Their hands touched, shyly. There

were half-humorous words exchanged which glowed with hidden meaning for the two, who had no eyes for anyone else in that enchanted room, no ears for any music now, but that which played within their own ears and eyes and hearts.

Romeo begged a kiss. Shyly, Juliet gave it. And then again, as though there was no time but this sweet moment, no place but that in which they stood together.

And then the world broke through and she was swept away in the broad encircling arms of Nurse to see her mother.

Who was she, this guest in Capulet's house? Romeo longed to know. But she was no guest, she was the only daughter of old Capulet.

Romeo's heart missed a beat. The only daughter of his father's enemy! Was he to stare at her across the chasm of hatred which split Montague from Capulet by a century of spilling blood?

Old Capulet, watching the masked Montagues prepare to leave, was far from fuelling this ancient war. He felt too filled with merry humour, for tonight young Paris had come to woo his daughter, Juliet!

Stay, he urged the Montagues, giving no sign that he knew who they were. But they set off, and Juliet, lingering to watch, sent Nurse to ask the stranger's name; and so she learned that it was Romeo, a Montague, the only son of her own family's greatest enemy.

'My only love sprung from my only hate!' she gasped, for a moment appalled by it. But she would not let this evening's magic be dimmed! She gave no eyes to anything but the masked stranger, who departed with a backward look of longing that answered her own.

Benvolio and Mercutio had left the party and seen Romeo go on ahead of them. Now they could find him nowhere. They called. They teased. 'Romeo! Madman! Passion! Lover!' Mercutio called. He tried to conjure him by all the tricks that he could muster: by Rosaline's bright eyes, by her high forehead and her scarlet lip (for they knew nothing of the swift flight of Romeo's old love and the instant birth of his new). But still Romeo was nowhere to be found, and so, rollicking with good cheer and bawdy humour, the two friends rolled on their way home.

Yet Romeo was near, and heard them. He had gone ahead and on an impulse leapt the wall into old Capulet's orchard. Shocked by this surge of daring, he hid from his friends' mockery. Now, in the darkness, he crouched down, not knowing why he stayed or what he hoped to do, but propelled by that same unseen power of fascination towards the house where dazzling Juliet lived.

It was as if the darkness was suddenly aflame, for Juliet stepped out on to her balcony, and then it seemed to Romeo's eyes as though she was the sun rising to flood the world with glorious light.

An impulse pushed him forward, then he held back. He struggled with the wish to run to her and then to hide in shyness and just drink in the wondrous vision.

Juliet, on her balcony, was unaware of watching eyes. She sighed loudly, for she was wrestling with the misery of knowing that her passionate stranger was a Montague.

'Deny your father,' she begged, as though Romeo lodged somewhere in the rustling tree-tops. 'Refuse your name! Or if you will not, be my love and I'll no longer be a Capulet. It is your name that is my enemy. Oh, be some other name!' she addressed the moon and stars. 'What's in a name! If we call a rose by any other name it would smell as sweet. So would Romeo were he not called Romeo. Romeo, throw off your name, and take all myself!' she cried, abandoning herself to this secret dialogue with unseen love.

Romeo broke from the shadow of the wall. 'Call me but love,' he cried, 'and I'll be new baptized, I will be Romeo no more!'

With a cry Juliet fled back into the shadows, aghast at being watched when she believed she was alone. But realizing who the secret visitor was, she stepped forward, timidly, peeped, grew bolder and moved to look down across the balcony wall and see him.

'If my family sees you, they will murder you,' she warned him, softly, but letting her eyes caress his face so warmly that he felt armed against any Capulet dagger.

So they stood there, bathed in the moonlight that silver-tipped the fruit-tree tops, drunk with their new-made vows of love. For Juliet's heart was yet untapped, and though she knew her father brewed a marriage with Paris for her, she was bewitched by this mysterious young man who had, unasked, pierced the seclusion of her life, broken all the boundaries that divided this ancient, hate-locked city, and crossed forbidden territory to her side. *This* was not a love wrapped up in good sense and handed to her by a father, mother, Nurse, or any other. *This* love was hers, and even as they gave their first vows to each other, it entered her soul with a fierce passion that would never leave her.

'My bounty is as boundless as the sea,' she cried. 'My love as deep; the more I give to you, the more I have, for both are infinite!'

Romeo knew he could live in the magic of this night for ever. It seemed as though he had drifted from a wilderness in which he ached always alone, a pilgrim in a thankless search for love: (how long it seemed to be since he had thought he ached for Rosaline!). But now it was as though his whole existence led towards this single night, and nothing could exist outside. All time was now, he and Juliet locked in their bond of faith; there was no future and no past, except with her.

Quickly, before the world intrude with the dawn and take from them anything of their sworn love, he hurried to a monastery outside the city walls to see the monk, Friar Lawrence, who knew him well.

The friar was shocked to find young Romeo already up, and quickly guessed he had not been to bed that night. But learning that this excess of energy was not devoted to the lovely Rosaline, he was amazed to hear another girl had stolen in to take her place. He shook his head. Young men's love did not lie truly in their hearts, but in their eyes! What a tide of tears had Romeo shed for Rosaline, and look now – forgotten!

Romeo would have no scoldings at his fickleness. He had a single-minded purpose now. With all the speed that he could muster, Friar Lawrence must marry him to Juliet, and marry them today!

The friar stared, half disbelieving what he heard. This doting youth was so changeable he could not keep up with him! Yet, watching Romeo prowl up and down in a restless torment of excitement, he hoped that perhaps some deeper flame now spurred his young friend on.

Well, perhaps he should perform this marriage for the youth. Perhaps Capulets and Montagues would even cancel out their hate when such a love could fly the boundary between them!

Benvolio and Mercutio were puzzled. They had not seen Romeo since he left the feast, and he had not gone home that night. Yet they knew that Tybalt, the angry Capulet, had sent a letter to Romeo's house challenging him to a duel for insolence in coming to their ball!

'Romeo will answer it,' said Benvolio, certain of his cousin.

'Alas, poor Romeo!' mourned Mercutio, clasping his heart. 'He is already dead, stabbed with a young girl's black eye, shot through the ear with a love-song . . . And is he a man to encounter Tybalt?'

'Why, what is Tybalt?' Benvolio enquired.

'More than a prince of cats, I can tell you,' Mercutio waxed lyrical in scorn. 'He is the very butcher of a silk button, a duellist, a gentleman of the very first house, a man of fancy thrusts and lunges,' and he mimicked the self-important prancing steps of Tybalt.

But here came Romeo to interrupt their joke. And what a change there was! No longer the mooning youth of yesterday, but the Romeo of old, so quick and apt to exchange the cut and thrust of jest with them that Mercutio retired, defeated, from the contest, pleased to see his friend so thoroughly repaired in spirits. And so they strolled on, chatting, while Romeo nursed his precious secret knowledge and looked for some messenger from Juliet, for she had said that she would send one.

And here came Nurse, puffing across the square, fanning away the steaming heat, and pressing on, for though she knew that Capulet had already promised Juliet to Paris, her old heart warmed to this tale of secret love and she thrilled to be Juliet's messenger to Romeo.

Entrusted in the care of Nurse, then, Romeo sent word to Juliet. She must find some way to come to Friar Lawrence's cell that very afternoon. There the holy friar would marry them at once.

Juliet paced up and down as though every minute was an hour and every hour a day until she heard from Romeo. A thousand terrors filled her heart: perhaps Nurse had not yet found him; perhaps she brought bad news; perhaps he'd changed his mind and did not love her . . .

But when she heard the news all terrors fled, and only the prospect of her union with Romeo lived in her mind. So many hours to go till then!

At Lawrence's cell, Romeo awaited her arrival with scarcely less intensity of hope: there was no sorrow could undo the joy he won from one short minute in Juliet's sight. 'Then love-devouring death do what he dare!' he defied the world. 'It is enough I may call her mine!'

'These violent delights have violent ends,' the friar chided him, 'and in their triumph, they die. Love moderately,' he warned.

But when Juliet came, with an airy step that floated on the cushion of her love, the friar's misgivings were instantly dispelled. Truly these young people loved!

'Come,' he hurried them, 'and we will make short work.' They must be married now, for such a pair should not be held apart.

The heat hung leaden in the streets, damp, cloying, maddening.

Benvolio was nervous, for Mercutio was in a brazen mood, his wit stung to an irritable edge; and there were Capulets drifting through the streets looking for a fight. 'I pray you, good Mercutio, let's go in,' he begged. 'These hot days the mad blood is stirring.'

'Come, come, you are as hot in your mood as any in Italy,' Mercutio said restlessly, 'and as soon moved to be moody.'

'By my head, here come the Capulets,' Benvolio muttered.

'By my heel, I do not care,' retorted Murcutio, and turned his back on the approaching group.

'Gentlemen,' cried Tybalt, recognizing them as friends of Romeo, 'a word with one of you.'

'But one word with one of us?' said Mercutio, bristling. 'Couple it with something; make it a word and a blow!'

Benvolio tried to pull him back: away, into some private place to have their quarrel, for here all men's eyes were on them, and the prince had forbidden such brawling on pain of the heaviest punishment!

But Tybalt had lost interest in this sparring match, for he saw Romeo enter the square. 'Romeo!' he yelled. 'You are a villain!'

Romeo was fresh from his marriage to Juliet; he knew nothing of the challenge from this cousin of hers and he could find no anger in his heart even to rebuff the open venom of the words. 'I am no villain,' he spoke mildly. 'Therefore, farewell. I see you do not know me.'

'Boy,' spat Tybalt, ripe with insults, 'this shall not excuse the injuries you have done me. Therefore turn and draw your weapon!'

'I do protest,' persisted Romeo, 'I never injured you.' Even now his head was filled with nothing other than his marriage; it made him now a cousin to this Tybalt who pranced so desperately in search of a war. 'So, good Capulet, which name I hold as dearly as my own . . .'

Mercutio turned on his friend in disbelief. What had become of him,

so calmly, so *dishonourably* to submit to this puppet duellist's
taunts? Well, he would take the wretched insult up!

'Tybalt, you rat-catcher,' he yelled, and drew his sword.
And suddenly there they were, circling like wild cats . . .
'What would you have with me?' snarled Tybalt.

'Good king of cats, nothing but one of
your nine lives . . . ' jeered Mercutio.

'Gentle Mercutio, put your sword
away,' urged Romeo.

'Come sir,' Mercutio egged Tybalt on.

'Tybalt, Mercutio, the prince expressly
has forbidden fighting in Verona streets,'
Romeo cried out. 'Hold Tybalt! Good
Mercutio!' and he stepped towards his
friend to beat his weapon down. Swiftly
Tybalt's sword shot beneath his
uplifted arm and into Mercutio's side.

Mercutio clutched the wound. 'What,
are you hurt?' gasped Romeo.

'Aye, aye, a scratch, a scratch,' winced
Mercutio, and turned suddenly very pale.
'Go fetch a surgeon,' he breathed, grey
with pain.

'Courage, man,' urged Romeo, 'the hurt
cannot be much.'

'No, it is not so deep as a well, nor so wide as a
churchdoor, but it is enough, it will serve . . . Ask for me
tomorrow and you shall find me a grave man.' Mercutio
gasped, and staggered a little, reaching for Benvolio's arm.
'I am done for this world,' he cried. 'A plague on both your
houses! A dog, a rat, a mouse, a cat to scratch a man to
death!' he yelled at Tybalt. 'Why the devil did you come
between us, Romeo? I was hurt under your arm.'

In stricken misery, Romeo stared at his friend. 'I thought
all for the best,' he whispered. The black hatred that was so
swiftly stealing Mercutio's life now seemed to gather about
Romeo and push him on, and with a cry of fury for Mercutio he
leapt on Tybalt, fighting with a demon passion before he could
think again; and before the onslaught, murderous Tybalt fell dead.

Romeo looked at his bloody sword. He looked at Benvolio's white-faced panic, urging him to fly before the prince should come, for it was death for anyone who broke Verona's peace.

'Oh, I am fortune's fool,' gasped Romeo. Wed to Juliet only an hour ago, and now the killer of his wife's cousin! Love and Juliet should be beckoning him, now only death or flight could wave him on!

Even as he fled the square, the Prince of Verona came with soldiers, and with Montague and Capulet. Bitterly these enemies demanded justice for their side. 'For blood of ours, shed blood of Montague,' raged Juliet's mother. 'I beg for justice, which you, prince, must give. Romeo killed Tybalt. Romeo must not live!'

The prince looked at her in silent anger. *Mercutio* was no Capulet or Montague felled by their hatred! He was the prince's kinsman. He should have been beyond the reach of this vile feud. Would this poison *never* end? From now on he would be deaf to all the pleas these Capulets and Montagues used so easily to excuse the bitter fruits of enmity! As Romeo had been stung to this brawl by Mercutio's death, so would he reduce the sentence of death: but to a punishment no less complete.

Romeo was banished from Verona for ever more, on pain of instant death should he return.

Juliet knew nothing of the fight. She knew only that she loved, and that night would bring her husband to her bed.

'Come, gentle night,' she coaxed, 'come, loving, black-browed night. Give me my Romeo; and, when he shall die, take him and cut him out in little stars and he will make the face of heaven so fine that all the world will be in love with night . . .'

She turned eagerly to Nurse, who seemed to bring some news. But there was something wrong! No joyous ecstasy at imminent wedding nights from Nurse, but wringing hands, and wailing words! 'Tybalt dead and Romeo banished!'

Banished! Juliet struggled to understand the word. 'To speak that word is as if father, mother, Tybalt, Romeo, Juliet, were all dead. "Romeo is *banished!*" ' she cried. The man she longed to see, to love, to hold, gone from Verona for ever more!

At Friar Lawrence's cell Romeo too heard the prince's sentence on him. And he knew that banishment meant death, for it was banishment from Juliet, from life itself!

The friar spoke calming words: banishment was only banishment from Verona! 'Be patient,' he urged. 'The world is broad and wide.'

'There is no world without Verona walls,' cried Romeo.

'This is dear mercy from the prince,' protested Lawrence.

'It is torture,' wildly Romeo rejected it. 'Heaven is here, where Juliet lives, and every cat and dog and little mouse may live here in heaven and look on her, but Romeo may not!'

In vain the friar tried to calm his black despair, but Romeo would hear none of it. What could the friar know? He was not young, in love with Juliet, married a short hour, killer of Tybalt, and now *banished*. What could the friar know of such depths of hopelessness?

But now Nurse came hurrying in with messages from Juliet. She waited in desperate loneliness to see Romeo before he had to go. Nurse and Lawrence urged him to go to her; but he must leave for Mantua before the dawn. And then the friar would make his marriage to Juliet known, try to reconcile the families and obtain a pardon from the prince, so that Romeo could come back to bask in happiness!

His spirits much revived by this hopeful plan, and armed with the friar's promise that he would send word to Romeo in Mantua, of Juliet, in Verona, Romeo went to meet his love.

Capulet was worried by the grief that seemed to seize his daughter at Tybalt's death. Knowing nothing of the secret marriage to Romeo, he could not guess the true cause of her unhappiness, and he thought it sprang from far too deep a well of sorrow. He was anxious for his daughter's health, and wished to have her misery gone. What better way than to occupy her mind with being wed! What better way than to have her married, and quickly, too, to Paris! Having so made up his mind, he picked the day and told it to his astounded wife. On Thursday next, in two short days, Juliet would marry Paris.

'Go to Juliet, before you go to bed,' he told Lady Capulet. 'Prepare her, wife, for this wedding day.'

But Juliet was already locked in her wedding night with her new husband, longingly denying the birdsongs of the dawn that would take him away from her.

'I must be gone and live, or stay and die,' murmured Romeo, yet hoping she would entice him back for one last minute of happiness.

'That light is not daylight,' she whispered back. 'I know it, I. It is some meteor that the sun throws out to be your torchbearer and light you on your way to Mantua.'

'I have more care to stay than will to go! Come death, and welcome,'
Romeo cried, and folded her inside his arms.

But already the sky was paling and with the anxious arrival of Nurse,
come to hurry them along, he pulled away and began to climb down
from the balcony into the orchard. Was it just one short day ago that
he had first exchanged his love with Juliet? He seemed now to have
known her all his life!

He saw her pale face looking down and heard her paler whisper. 'Do
you think that we shall ever meet again? Oh god, I think I see you, now
you are below, as one dead in the bottom of a tomb! You look so pale.'

'And trust me, love, so do you. Dry sorrow drinks our blood.'

And then he was gone, nothing but the echoes of the night
still in her ears and on her lips and in her arms.

A call startled her. Lady Capulet was at her door! Why
was she up at this strange hour? So late not to be in bed:
so early to be up already!

Lady Capulet had much to tell, despite the hour: she had
a scheme to follow Romeo, the killer of Tybalt, to Mantua
with poison. Soon, he too would die. And other tidings which
she delivered with all the certainty of Juliet's pleasure: in two
days time she would be wed to Paris!

Juliet heard it through a mask: she let no look or word escape
to tell of her love for Tybalt's killer, nor that she was a wife before
ever Paris could lay claim on her. Half in terror at the trap she saw, half
in terror at her parents' anger when they knew, she cried, 'I wonder at
this haste! I pray you, tell my father that I will not marry yet.'

'Here comes your father; tell him so yourself and see how he will
take it at your hands!' her mother told her angrily.

'What, still in tears?' her father demanded brusquely. He turned on
his wife in irritation.

'Have you delivered to her our decree?'

'Aye, sir, but she will none. She gives you thanks. I wish the fool
were married to her grave!'

'How!' bellowed Capulet. 'Is she not proud? Does she not count her
blessings, unworthy that she is, that we have brought so worthy a
gentleman to be her bridegroom?'

'Not proud you have,' protested Juliet, in tears, 'but thankful that
you have . . .'

'How now, how now! What is this?' her father yelled. ' "Proud" and

"I thank you" and "I thank you not". Thank me no thankings nor proud me no prouds, but prepare yourself for Thursday next to go with Paris to St Peter's Church or I will drag you on a hurdle!'

'Good father, I beg you,' wept Juliet, 'hear me with patience.'

'Disobedient wretch! I tell you what: get to church on Thursday or never after look me in the face: speak not, reply not, do not answer me; my fingers itch! God's bread,' raged Capulet. 'It makes me mad: day, night, hour, tide, time, work, play, alone, in company, all my care has been to have her married: and having now provided a suitable gentleman, to have her answer, "I'll not wed, I cannot love, I am too young, I pray you, pardon me!" I do not jest,' he hissed at her, 'if you will not wed, you may hang, beg, starve, die in the streets, for by my soul I'll never take you in!'

Juliet sat trembling in the silence behind his departing back.

'Oh, sweet mother, cast me not away,' she begged. 'Delay this marriage for a month, a week; or if you do not, make my bridal bed in that dim monument of death where Tybalt lies!'

'Talk not to me,' her mother waved her off, 'for I'll not speak a word. Do as you will, for I have done with you.'

Juliet sank beneath a tide of hopelessness. All helping hands withdrawn! All roads to Romeo cut off and only one path open – marriage to another man!

She fled to Friar Lawrence's cell. The friar trembled at the dangers now looming before them all. A desperate plan took shape within his brain, fraught with a kind of horror. But Juliet was ready for anything to keep her faith as Romeo's wife.

Friar Lawrence gave her a potion: drink it, and she would seem to die, while all the while she only slept. This sleep with the look of death would last for forty-two hours; so, when they came to rouse her for the wedding, they would think her dead! According to long-established custom, they would lay her body in the tomb where the bodies of all the Capulets lay.

Meantime, the friar would send word to Romeo in Mantua. Romeo would hurry to the tomb to greet her when she woke, and carry her away with him to safety!

Awash with sudden hope, Juliet seized the friar's potion and hurried to her room.

The household was in a flurry such as there had never been before. One more day to prepare a wedding feast! Old Capulet gave orders for the festivities, while watching for some change of heart in Juliet.

And so there seemed to be! She came from Friar Lawrence all smiles, begging his pardon, and saying she would now be ruled by him!

'Send for Paris,' Capulet roared in triumph. 'I'll have this knot knit up tomorrow morning.'

'No, not till Thursday,' Lady Capulet begged her headstrong husband. 'We will be short in our supplies: it's nearly night!'

But he would have no contradiction. 'We'll go to church tomorrow.' His heart soared, so light it felt now that his wayward daughter had seen the error of her ways.

Juliet was alone. The silence filled her with a faint cold fear, like the creeping chill of tombs to which she would shortly give herself. It almost froze the heat of life in her. So suddenly to be faced with this! No time to think!

A thousand fears grimaced in her mind: what if the friar's potion did not work? She seized her dagger and held it up: why then, this would have to do the task! What if she woke before she was rescued, trapped in a tomb with only dead people to keep her company? Perhaps the loathsome foulness of the air would strangle her, or send her mad . . .

She pushed the visions back, and with a rush of courage raised the potion. 'Romeo, I come,' she whispered to the silence. 'This I drink to you.'

In Mantua, Romeo knew nothing of all this. He neither knew of Friar Lawrence's secret potion to make Juliet seem dead, nor that her father insisted that she marry Paris now.

His servant brought him only the news that Juliet was dead, found lifeless on the morning of her marriage.

The words broke upon him like the ice of his own death.

'Is it really so?' he breathed. 'Then I defy you, stars! I will go there tonight . . .'

'Sir, have patience,' his servant begged. 'Your looks are pale and wild.'

Romeo brushed his worries off, and urged him away to find horses for the journey to Verona.

'Well, Juliet, I will lie with you tonight,' he told her, in his head. A plan had taken hold of him, and now he had no other purpose in his life. Quickly he found a man in Mantua to sell him a deadly poison. 'Come, poison,' he spoke softly to the fatal bottle in his hand. 'Go with me to Juliet's grave, for there I must use you.'

Friar Lawrence hurried to the tomb where Juliet lay, armed with an iron bar to open it. His heart pounded with misery and fright. The messenger sent to tell Romeo that Juliet was not dead, only asleep, had not reached him! Both messenger and letter had been put in quarantine against the plague, and only just released.

So now the friar hastened to reach Juliet. She would wake soon, alone, trapped in the tomb. He must rescue her before she died of fright! Then, he would write again to Romeo and keep Juliet in his cell until Romeo could come to take her.

'Poor living corpse,' he wept, 'closed in a dead man's tomb!' There was another visitor to the tomb that night. Paris knew nothing of Juliet's love for Romeo, nor of her terror at the marriage planned with him. He wept to lose her on their wedding day, and he came to lay flowers on the tomb and weep his private tears.

A third figure was entering the graveyard shadows. It was Romeo, fired by a grim light within which made his servant tremble.

'Whatever you hear or see, stand well away and do not interrupt me in my course,' Romeo gave orders to his servant. 'Do not return and pry, or by heaven I will tear you joint by joint and strew this hungry churchyard with your limbs!'

'I will be gone, sir, and not trouble you,' the servant hastily assured him. But he hid, to wait, for fear of what his desperate master planned.

Paris, sheltering behind the Capulet tomb, saw only that the Montague who had killed Juliet's cousin and made her take her life, now tried to open the tomb and desecrate it. With a shout of rage, he drew his sword and rushed to stop him.

And Romeo, knowing only that no one must stop him reaching Juliet's side, brought the intruder down.

'Oh, I am killed,' Paris gasped. 'If you be merciful, open the tomb and lay me with Juliet.'

Romeo saw now who he had killed, and understood that this man too loved Juliet. Sorrowfully, he lifted him and carried him into the tomb, and laid him gently on the floor.

Then he rose, and climbed on to the cold stone slab where Juliet lay, and knelt with her.

She lay so warmly beautiful. He did not see the crimson blush of her lips or fresh bloom of her cheeks as life, only as her beauty flaming for him even in her death. He could almost believe that Death itself loved her, and kept her in her glory here, to be his bride.

But Romeo would defy even Death, for he would stay with her and never leave this palace of dim night!

He lifted her then to his last embrace, sealed her lips with a kiss that would never end; and then he raised the poison to his lips and drank, and fell across her body, dead.

Friar Lawrence panted through the graveyard. He found Romeo's servant, and such a terror filled him as he had never known. He saw the bloodstains at the entrance to the tomb, the gory sword flung down, ran in and saw Romeo's lifeless corpse, and bloody Paris too.

Above this grim monument to death, Juliet began to stir. She saw the friendly face of Friar Lawrence, and smiled. 'Oh, comfortable friar, where is my lord? I do remember well where I should be, and here I am! But where is Romeo?'

Bereft of words, the friar shrank from the sight that greeted Juliet's waking eyes. He heard a noise outside, 'Lady, come from that nest of death,' he begged. 'Come, come away! Your husband lies there dead, and Paris too. Come, I'll put you in a sisterhood of holy nuns. Stay not to question,' he pleaded again. 'Good Juliet, I dare no longer stay.'

'Go,' said Juliet, 'for I will not away.'

A vast blackness filled her, as though the dark chill of death had already taken her. There was no world outside this place: no world beyond this tomb, where Romeo lay . . .

She found the cup of poison in his hand: no drop in it to help her on her way! She kissed his lips: no poison clung to them, only the warmth of life just gone.

But here his dagger waited, like a friend.

'Oh happy dagger!' she cried. 'This is your sheath!' and as the sounds of people running to the tomb broke in upon her world of timelessness, she stabbed herself and fell dead on Romeo, locked in her last embrace.

Capulet and Montague gathered around those they had buried with their hate. The sight of their children's deaths was like a bell that tolled their own deaths in this world of viciousness in which they revelled. And the sight of death was now the bell that tolled them back from it.

'Where be these enemies?' the Prince of Verona cried. 'Capulet! Montague! See what a scourge is laid upon your hate!' He looked at the body of Paris, so swiftly following Mercutio. 'And I too,' he mourned, 'for winking on your quarrels, have lost a brace of kinsmen. All are punished.'

But the tolling bell was heard by those who had till now heard nothing. Capulet reached a hand across to Montague. Each swore to raise a statue in pure gold in honour of the other's child; so would all know the tale of Romeo and Juliet, who fell before the venom of an ancient war, and only whose deaths had sounded the final call to peace.

Macbeth

The Witches   King Duncan   Malcolm   Donalbain
King of Scotland   *Duncan's sons*

Macbeth   Banquo   Lady Macbeth   Macduff
King Duncan's   *Macbeth's wife*   *the Thane of Fife, a*
Generals   *Scottish lord*

Sunless mists turned about the place, and rocks crouched low beneath a rumbling thunder. Into the circle of the gloom they came, twisting figures woven in the air; and with them came dark whisperings:

'When shall we three meet again, in thunder, lightning or in rain?'

Hoarse with a poisonous hate, the answer lingered.

'When the hurlyburly's done; when the battle's lost . . . and won.'

The sodden earth began to tremble . . .

'That will be before the set of sun.'

'Where the place?'

'Upon the heath.' A curdling wail rose through the air, as though a thousand wretched creatures were imprisoned in that moaning place.

'There to meet with *Macbeth!*' The final venomous shriek swept from the writhing shadows low across the heather and then up, up into the eye of a blackly gathering storm . . .

King Duncan's camp was bright and quick with movement. Men strode fast between low flickering fires and every hour the messengers sped from the battlefield towards the waiting king.

A soldier stumbled into camp, staggered, and fell. They saw the staring horror of a long-fought battle in his face and ropes of blood draining his filth-streaked limbs.

They raised him up and sent for dressings for the wounds, while battle-weary men gathered around.

Between hoarse, panting breaths the soldier spilled his tale: how bitterly the battle ebbed and flowed! Neither the soldiers of the king nor those of the rebel army were gaining ground, until . . . his voice broke, sobbed, and listeners drew closer, fearing the worst. It seemed the villainous rebel Macdonwald gained a hold and viciously pressed forward his attack! And then . . .

'Brave Macbeth! Well he deserves that name!' the soldier cried, and a new fire coursed through his limbs, as with his arms swung wide he showed the mighty swordsweeps of Macbeth. His listeners could almost see Macbeth carve his unflinching path through spear and axe.

'At last,' he said, 'Macbeth stood face to face against Macdonwald.' And now the soldier stood erect, as though he would draw Macbeth's great strength into his own battered limbs. And with gigantic swirling blows he showed how Macbeth battled Macdonwald towards his death. A mighty, final deathstroke the soldier gave, and there, before the watchers' eyes, the rebel Macdonwald fell.

'O valiant cousin!' King Duncan's voice shook. How could his gratitude for Macbeth's valour be weighed in words? It seemed that Scotland's fate, the people's lives, his own, were cradled in the vast courage of this warrior's breast.

'But mark, King of Scotland, mark,' the soldier swayed and a grey weariness drained his face. 'The King of Norway with new supplies of men began a fresh assault!'

'Did this dismay our generals, Macbeth and Banquo?' the King questioned urgently.

'Yes . . .' A sharp in-drawn breath hissed through the crowd. So the battle was now lost! The soldier drew up his trembling body and threw his shoulders wide. 'As sparrows would dismay the eagle or the hare dismay the lion!'

'Ah . . .' the single murmur of relief swept around, with nods and smiles. Even now they could see Macbeth and Banquo, fighting stroke for stroke against the enemy, their demon onslaught drawing other soldiers on with new-born strength! But now the soldier who told the tale grew faint, and sank to the ground.

'Your wounds tell of your honour, as do your words,' King Duncan said. 'Go, get him to the surgeons.'

He swung suddenly on his heel as a new commotion sounded at the gate. It was the Thane of Ross, hot-foot from the battlefield. He sped through the camp towards them. 'God save the King!' he cried. 'The King of Norway himself, helped by that disloyal traitor the Thane of Cawdor, began a dismal conflict! Until our general, Macbeth, like the unvanquished God of War, confronted him sword point against point, arm against arm . . .' The thane's voice soared with triumph, 'and, to conclude, the victory fell on us!'

'Great happiness!' King Duncan's voice broke. He raised his arms silently, as though to encircle every loyal man. The bloody course of battle was now run and all the rebels were in flight. His aged shoulders straightened, as though finally he threw off a weighty burden. What rich rewards were owed by him to loyal men! He sighed: so too was punishment owed to the rebel lord who joined with an invading king.

Swiftly he gave commands. Traitors would no more betray this land: *death* would be the payment for that Thane of Cawdor's treachery.

'And with the traitor's title,' triumphantly the king announced, 'greet Macbeth.' His voice grew sombre. 'What Cawdor has lost, noble Macbeth has won!' With these words King Duncan's hand rose up, slowly, as though the great Macbeth were cradled in his royal grasp.

Storm clouds swelled above the heath. The last rim of light lingered, hopelessly, and then was smothered.

At the crossroads, the air grew heavy. Gorsebushes and blackened tree stumps trembled. Darkness sank, thick and dark and oily; and from its centre a reeking vapour coiled, snaked upward from the earth, spiralled and spread . . .

Within, three figures moved: twisted forms of wizened skin and knotted hair. Locked one to the other in a grimly rhythmic sway they turned, now this way, now the other, the murmur of their chant like some fiendish heartbeat in the rising howl of winds.

Above the gale a drumbeat boomed. The figures paused, and swivelled towards the sound and a glow of ugly glee inflamed their watching faces.

Macbeth and Banquo trod a weary path across the heath, and with resounding drumbeat Banquo killed the memories of horror on the field of war.

Macbeth walked deep in thought. He shrugged his shoulders high against the winds.

Banquo's drumbeat stopped. Into their faces rose a stench as though a rottenness steamed from the caverns of a poisonous earth. Three withered forms rose to their gaze: gnarled skeletons of rag and bone sheathed in a bloody light. Each raised a crooked finger to skinny lips.

Macbeth shivered. An iciness seeped through his bones. He summoned all his will.

'Speak if you can! What are you?' His command rose into the wind.

One grisly figure rasped a crackling chant:

'All hail Macbeth! hail to thee, Thane of Glamis!'

Another, 'All hail, Macbeth! hail to thee, Thane of Cawdor!'

The words hung in the rancid air. In that moment, waiting, Macbeth felt a coiling in his stomach, as though a serpent writhed . . .

'All hail, Macbeth! that shalt be king hereafter!'

In the warrior's heart there was a hammering as though his ribs would break. King!

To be king!

Banquo moved towards the apparitions. 'If you can look into the seeds of time, and say which grain will grow, and which will not, speak then to me . . .'

'Hail!' the creaking voices rose to a crescendo.

'Lesser than Macbeth, and greater.'

'Not so happy, yet much happier.'

'Thou shalt get kings, though thou be none!'

Macbeth broke across their rhythm. 'Tell me more: I know I am Thane of Glamis; but how of Cawdor? The Thane of Cawdor lives . . .' he paused, 'and to be king . . .' It was beyond belief. How could they know? What more might they foresee?

'Speak!' he cried, more urgently, but already the gory glow that held the monstrous trio began to seep into the sodden ground; their forms began to melt. Only the odour of decay hung in the leaden air.

Macbeth and Banquo were alone again.

'Your children shall be kings,' murmured Macbeth.

'*You* shall be king,' Banquo's voice betrayed the wonder of his half-belief.

Macbeth's thoughts churned. There *is* a king: There *is* a Thane of Cawdor. The storm shrieked the words into a thundering pattern inside his head.

'Who's here?' At Banquo's sudden cry, two men broke through the gloom towards them, breathless with the burden of their news: the fame of Macbeth's battle deeds had reached the king and they now brought the monarch's thanks to him.

And yet their words were almost lost, for he was hearing other voices in the wind. Until the words '*the Thane of Cawdor*' pierced his thoughts: the Thane of Cawdor had been judged a traitor, and as thanks for Macbeth's services in war, and sign of honours yet to come, the king *now gave Macbeth that name.*

The prophecy! Already one part true.

What of the other part? Before his eyes there rose an image of the king. Bold, strong, alive.

Yet *I* should be king. The hammering in his ribs grew stronger. Hair rose across his scalp, as though some dreadful thought was searching for a nesting place within his brain.

And yet, the image was already there.

The vision of a single, bloody act.

To kill the king.

The thought swelled, and became alive, and Macbeth struggled to push it back.

'Come friends,' he forced himself to say, 'let us towards the king . . .'

In the palace the king awaited news. Had Cawdor been executed yet? The business troubled him.

'He was a gentleman on whom I built an absolute trust,' he murmured to Malcolm, his son. He sighed: how little of what a person really thought was written on their face! He grew weary with this sorrow; his trust had been so painfully misplaced.

There was a sudden commotion in the Court and cries of jubilant welcome. Macbeth and Banquo had come! The king rose swiftly to meet them: such true men they were, throwing their lives behind their loyalty to Scotland and her king!

'O worthiest cousin!' his heart overflowed with all he owed Macbeth: more, more than ever he could pay.

Macbeth stood, great and battle-stained before his king.

'Our duties,' he paused, beating back a thousand whirling thoughts, 'our duties are to your throne and state. We do only what we should, by doing everything to ensure your safety, love and honour.'

For a long, silent moment, the king grasped his hand. 'Welcome! You are welcome here!'

And now he turned to Macbeth's staunch companion.

'Noble Banquo! You have deserved no less.' Warmly he embraced his general, and turned away to wipe the joyful tears which now flowed freely down his cheeks.

Then he swung with sudden resolution to face the waiting Court. 'Sons, kinsmen, thanes,' he said, steadying his voice, 'know that I now declare as heir to my throne and state . . .'

Macbeth looked up, a quickening pulse beating below his temple. So soon! The final prophecy!

And yet the king was moving past and placing a hand upon the shoulder of his son!

'. . . my eldest, Malcolm. We name him heir to the throne and Prince of Cumberland.'

A mist of whispering thoughts leapt to Macbeth's brain. He was not to be the future king, but the king's son, Malcolm, would be instead!

That is a step, he breathed, on which I must fall down, or else . . . he searched for his answer, and a restless anguish coiled within him: the serpent of ambition writhed – he recognized it fully now. He saw the crown on Duncan's head burning as a beacon to draw him on. He *would* be king.

'Stars, hide your fires. Let not light see my black and deep desires.'

The lady lifted the letter to the flickering light and read again. A strange tale, her lord Macbeth told her! Bewitched encounters on the heath; glorious honours foretold. The letter breathed fire into her very limbs, and answered an inward flame.

She seemed to see her husband stand before her, tall and strong.

'Glamis you are, and Cawdor,' she murmured, 'and you shall be what you are promised.'

And yet, she saw him too, too clearly. 'I do fear your nature. It is too full of the milk of human kindness.' How well she knew that! He wanted greatness, power, wealth; but would not willingly play falsely for it. He yearned for that which was not his; and yet he would not do what *must* be done, to win.

'Macbeth,' she longed to see him. 'Hurry to me, that I may pour my courage in your ear . . .' There was a sudden movement at the door. A messenger! She turned urgently to hear his news.

'The king comes here tonight,' he said.

'Tonight!' She signalled him away and turned, to gaze far into the distance beyond the castle walls.

Tonight! She closed her eyes. Deep within her lungs, her stomach, her loins, she drew breath, as though she would suck the fires from the centre of the earth.

'Come you spirits that wait on human thoughts,' she cried, 'fill me from crown to toe top-full of direst cruelty! Make thick my blood . . . come, come, thick night . . .'

Tonight they would begin the climb towards the crown. Tonight they would kill the king. She saw the crown now shining only for them . . .

It was there Macbeth found her, and wordlessly they clung together.

'My dearest love,' he murmured then, not looking in her eyes, 'Duncan comes here tonight,' and he turned restlessly to avoid her gaze.

She seized his face and swung it towards her, and her hand was steel.

'You shall put this night's business into *my* care.'

Hastily Macbeth drew back from her, lowering his eyes. 'We will speak further.'

'Only look up!' she urged. 'Leave all the rest to me!'

The royal party came at dusk: the king and his two sons, Malcolm and Donalbain; Banquo and all the noble lords. Their mood was light. The fruits of victory against the enemy were now secured, and it gave to all of them a pleasant lack of care. They marvelled at the sweet summer air that flowed so softly about Macbeth's castle. And how warmly did his lady welcome them into her home! Words of honour and loving debt flowed from her lips, and in the evening she prepared a sumptuous banquet for her royal guests.

It pleased King Duncan well. The castle halls rang with the joyful sound of music; servants flew to and fro; great dishes steamed with the rich odours of succulent foods and torches flamed a merry welcome.

Only Macbeth left the festivities, suddenly, and sought the dark. Alone in the courtyard, he strode to and fro.

What visions bedevilled his tired brain! If only such deeds as he imagined could be swiftly done, and ended there. But could there ever be rest again after the murder of a king? Could there ever be sleep again after the killing of a man so gracious, noble, kind, as Duncan?

'He's here in double trust,' he told himself. 'First, as I am his cousin and his subject; and then, as I am his host, who should shut the door against his murderer, not bear the knife myself.'

And yet the serpent coiled within him still. To be king! To rule all Scotland!

Lady Macbeth came searching for him, angrily.

'We'll go no further in this business,' he said to her.

Such scorn she spat at him, he winced beneath its lash!

'Are you afraid?'

'Peace,' Macbeth struggled against her rage. 'I dare do all that is fitting for a man.'

'What beast was it then, that made you break this enterprise to me? When you *dared* do it, *then* you were a man!'

He strove to find another reason against the deed: 'If we should fail?'

'We fail! But screw your courage to the sticking place and we'll not fail!' She stood before him, certain in her power. And step by step, she laid her deadly plan before him: Duncan's servant would be overpowered with wine and fall into a drunken stupor. 'What cannot you and I perform upon the unguarded Duncan then?'

Her certainties lulled him. The bloody visions stilled.

It was all settled, now.

They stood together, each with a private vision of the golden promises to come. Each bone and sinew must be steeled and bent to do this horrible thing. Macbeth prepared.

He waited, shrouded in the darkness of the court. The revelry was over and all the guests were in bed; Macbeth alone listened for the bell to call him to the night's grim task.

How long those minutes were until that dread bell's note!

He looked into the shadows, moving with an uneasy tread. And then he halted, staring, aghast.

'Is this a dagger which I see before me, the handle towards my hand?' He tried to seize the weapon, but his fingers passed through air. And still the blade hung there!

And now it dripped with blood!

He stumbled back against the stair that led towards the king.

'There's no such thing,' he cried. 'It is this bloody business which brings it to my eyes!'

Against the wall, he felt the hardness of the stone along his back. This wall was real. So was the earth on which he stood. He braced himself and stilled his trembling mind.

The bell! Far off it tolled. The summons from his wife coursed through his body like a fire, and drew him on, on up the stair, towards the sleeping king . . .

His wife came into the blanketing gloom within the court. She had drunk some of the wine that she had given to King Duncan's guards and it had fired her inward flame.

She was now ready.

She strained her ears towards the rooms beyond the stairs.

'He is about it.'

She listened again. 'I laid their daggers ready; he could not miss them!' But what if the guards awoke before Macbeth had killed the king? She raised her hands against her face. They trembled, and she had not known they would.

She thought then of the king, asleep, at peace, as she had seen him only a few moments ago, and a sudden ache stirred through her. 'Had he not looked like my father as he slept, I would have done it.'

A shuffling lurch came on the stair above! Macbeth swayed there, ashen-faced.

'I have done the deed,' he whispered. 'Did you not hear a noise?'

'I heard the owl scream and the crickets cry,' she answered him. 'Did you not speak?'

'When?'

'Now.'

'As I descended?' he searched the darkness beyond her.

'Ay,' she moved towards him.

He pulled away and stared at his bloody hands. 'This is a sorry sight.'

'A foolish thought to say a sorry sight!' she retorted angrily.

He raised his eyes and looked into her face, and what eyes they were!

And then he froze, as though somewhere within the winds that gathered round their towers he'd heard a sound. He pointed a trembling finger, 'I thought I heard a voice cry "Sleep no more, Macbeth has murdered sleep." '

'What do you mean?' she cried.

He stumbled to the window, 'Still it cried "Sleep no more! . . . Glamis has murdered sleep, and therefore Cawdor shall sleep no more; Macbeth shall sleep no more!" '

She seized his arm, and she was scornful now.

'Go, get some water and wash this filthy witness from your hand.' In horror she seized the blades clutched in his fingers. 'Why did you bring these daggers from the place? They must lie there: go carry them.'

'I'll go no more!' Macbeth gasped, hoarse, 'I am afraid to think what I have done. Look on it again, I dare not.'

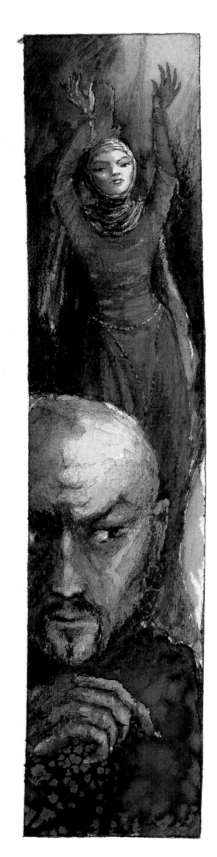

'Give me the daggers!' She sped up the stairs. And if the king was bleeding, why, she would smear his blood across the guards and everyone would see that it was they who had done this thing!

A thunderous knocking boomed across the court. Macbeth shuddered, and did not move.

'What hands are here? They pluck out my eyes! All great Neptune's ocean will not wash this blood clean from my hand!'

She had returned, and now her hands too reeked with Duncan's blood! He recoiled in horror as she held them up. 'My hands are of your colour, but I shame to wear a heart so white!' she said.

Again the knocking thundered. She urged his attention, pulling him towards their rooms. 'A little water clears us of this deed. How easy it is then!' The knocking came again. 'Hark! Get on your nightgown.'

As though he saw the hammer of doom beyond, Macbeth stared wretchedly at the outer door. 'Wake Duncan with this knocking! I wish you could!'

It was Macduff, the noble Thane of Fife who came with other lords to wake the king. They hammered at the castle door and shivered in the bitter morning chill. How warm the summer bloom of evening air had been the night before; and yet what storms had torn the sky since then! The wind had seemed to scream with agony, and trembling, like a fever, shook the earth.

Macbeth greeted them, dressed in his nightgown and told them the king was not yet up.

'I'll bring you to him,' Macbeth said.

He led Macduff towards the room. The thane went in. There was a moment as he crossed the floor, a pause, a strangled gasp, and then a cry that pierced the very stones around them.

'O horror, horror, horror! Awake, awake!' Macduff's voice rang throughout the castle. 'Murder and treason! Banquo and Donalbain! Malcolm! Awake!'

Bells rang, torches flamed and the castle echoed with running feet.

Lady Macbeth hurried to them: what hideous thing had so alarmed her guests?

'Our royal master's murdered!'

Who? Who had done it? His guards! Bathed in the king's blood, confused and babbling, their filthy daggers lying on their pillows.

But Macbeth, in fury for the murder of his king, it seemed, had taken swift revenge and killed them instantly!

'Why did you do so?' Macduff exclaimed. It startled him. So swiftly to kill those they could question about the night's unnatural events: their punishment was too hastily done!

Or was it? A grain was seeded in Macduff's mind, even as he heard the words of grief spilling from Macbeth's lips. He watched him. And Lady Macbeth watched Macduff.

Could this bold thane already see the lies that lurked below the surface of her husband's words? Did he suspect Macbeth had killed the guards to stop them talking?

'Help me!' she swayed, as though about to faint.

'Look to the lady,' Macduff commanded. They rushed to help her. And no one else, it seemed, had seen what he had seen.

Within the hour Malcolm and Donalbain sped from the castle. It seemed to Malcolm that the murderer of a king would turn next to the murder of the sons and heirs to that king's throne. Here, for them, there were daggers in men's smiles.

The dark spirits of the heath had sowed their poisonous seed and what rich soil it had found! How it had grown and fruited!

And now the crop was nearly in: King Duncan dead and Malcolm, the heir to the throne, in flight. It seemed to everyone that it must prove his guilt: he must have bribed the guards to murder his own father.

The nobles sought a new heir to the throne of Scotland. Macbeth! So loyal and honest a cousin to king Duncan; and had he not in battle proved his love for Scotland and her king?

And so Macbeth took up the crown, and no one could deny so worthy a man ascending to Duncan's royal seat.

Except Macduff, the noble Thane of Fife. He did not attend the coronation of Macbeth, but watched it from afar, and wondered.

Banquo remained, adviser to Macbeth. But such cursed thoughts he'd had since that dark day upon the heath, and such vile dreams now mocked his sleep!

He thought of the new-made king, Macbeth. 'You have it now,' he murmured. 'King, Cawdor, Glamis, all as the weird women promised, and I fear you played most foully for it.'

But had they not also said that he would be root and father of many kings? The promise beckoned him, and yet his nature struggled with the poison of the witches' words, and deep within, he knew how Macbeth had taken the crown . . .

Macbeth came to him, richly dressed in royal robes and attended by his queen, the lords and nobles of the Court. He announced, 'Tonight, we hold a ceremonial supper, sir, and I request your presence.'

'Let your highness command me,' Banquo replied. Each minute his distance from this man who was his friend seemed to get wider.

'Will you ride this afternoon?' Macbeth enquired. 'Is it far you ride?'

'As far, my lord, as will fill up the time between now and supper.'

The king nodded, thoughtfully. 'Fail not our feast.' And he watched Banquo go, taking his young son with him. This man now woke a fear in Macbeth's breast that clawed deep as a dagger's blade.

'There is no one but he whose being I do fear,' he thought. Brave, wise Banquo: he knew of the dark women on the heath, and of their promises. And had they not hailed him as father to a line of kings? 'To *me* they did not speak of heirs: no son will follow *me* on to the throne.'

The barren prospect chilled Macbeth with a new and terrifying pain. To have dredged up such evil from within his soul; to have stilled all the warmth of loyalty, honour, love, humanity! And all for what?

'Then I have defiled my mind for Banquo's sons. For them I have murdered the gracious Duncan. For Banquo's heirs I have given up my soul to the dark spirits and surrendered sleep to the shuddering visions of these endless nights . . .'

The agony worked deep within him, bending him towards new avenues of hate. He sent for cloaked, hidden men with scowling desperation on their faces. And in their hands Macbeth now laid the lives of Banquo and his son. This threat to him *would* end; snuffed like a candle even as they rode towards his feast.

And all the while the queen roamed listlessly. A drugging weariness now bedevilled every step she took. All had seemed so simple when she planned it: the crown was so near at hand, so easy for the taking, and the murder of a man so quick, so neatly done.

And yet what was it worth, now that they had it all?

'My lord, why do you keep alone?' she questioned Macbeth again. She ached to stand with him as once she had, when that shining thread of their ambition had woven them together. 'What's done is done,' she pleaded, but her words fell on stony ground.

'We have scorched the snake, not killed it,' he retorted sharply. Could she not see the snake would return to rip his nights with poisoned tooth?

These dreams that nightly tortured him!

'So full of scorpions is my mind, dear wife!' he said to her.

'Gentle my love,' she tried to touch his face. 'Be bright and jovial among your guests tonight.'

In a dark place near the palace Macbeth's murderers did their swift butcher's work and sliced the life from Banquo. But Banquo's son escaped and fled into the night.

In the palace the ceremonial feast was laid: a royal banquet to hail a new-crowned king. Macbeth played monarch with gracious words, welcoming his guests and preparing to drink a toast to them.

There was a sudden movement. The murderer came to the door with blood smeared on his face, and hastily Macbeth went to him. Was Banquo dead? Yes, his throat was cut, and twenty deep gashes on his head. His son? His son had fled!

The fear swelled in him like the last wave that would drown him as he stood. He braced himself, and turned towards the celebration feast, summoning the smilings of a host on to his face. The lords hailed him to sit with them.

'The table's full,' he said. He could not see an empty place to sit. Even where they showed him there was a place, there was a man . . .

But it was not a man! It was the tatters of a man, all gashed and soaked with blood, his head half-hanging from his gaping neck . . . it stared at him, and stared . . . Macbeth cried, 'You cannot say I did it. Never shake your gory locks at me!'

The nobles leapt in consternation to their feet; the queen urged them to sit again.

'Shame!' she hissed at trembling Macbeth. 'Why do you make such faces? When all's done, you look but on a stool!' He looked, and it was gone. He straightened up and breathed again.

'The time has been that, when the brains were out, the man would die, and there an end,' he assured the startled Court. 'But now they rise again and push us from our stools!'

The queen seized his arm. Had he lost all his sense? The nobles would hear and know what they had done! She urged him towards the

feast. He strained to hold his mind and body firm, and once more he approached the table.

Again! Banquo! All pale and bloody, and staring with sightless eyes! He tried to shield himself, 'How can you behold such sights,' he accused the watching nobles, 'and keep the natural ruby of your cheeks when mine are blanched with fear?'

'What sights, my lord?' a thane enquired of him.

'I pray you, speak not,' the queen pleaded. 'He is not well. Question enrages him. Stand not upon the order of your going, but go at once!'

They went. But they had heard.

'It will have blood,' Macbeth murmured wretchedly. 'They say blood will have blood.'

His wife stood watching him. There was no life left in her now. All was spent. She saw how far beyond her reach he now had moved! Sleep beckoned her, only sleep. How long was it since she, or he, had slept?

Macbeth's brain fastened on a new thought. Macduff! He had not come to celebrate. Macduff refused to celebrate his kingship Macbeth knew, for did he not keep spies in every noble's court? Did he not need them to sniff out hidden treacheries that rose against a king! Fears pressed down on him from every side and hemmed him in. Suddenly he made up his mind. 'I will tomorrow, early, go to the weird sisters. More shall they speak, for now I am bent to know, by the worst means, the worst. For my own good, all others shall give way! I wade so deep in blood already that returning would be as wretched as going on!'

Now the strange behaviour of the king was known, and far and wide the people talked of it. They said that he was mad, and whispered of the bloody path by which he had mounted to the throne.

It was also known that Malcolm had received a royal welcome in England, at King Edward's court. There also Macduff, the Thane of Fife, had gone, to ask the English king for help. He said that Malcolm, the rightful heir to Duncan, should come against Macbeth, the murdering usurper of the royal throne of Scotland.

Macbeth learned of these moves against him, and prepared.

He found the twisted women of the heath in a deep cavern, brooding like vultures above a cauldron's steam. They swayed and moaned and threw some vile, rotting thing into the bilious brew, and grimly their chant rose above the cauldron's hiss.

'Round about the cauldron go
In the poisoned entrails throw.

Double, double toil and trouble;
Fire burn and cauldron bubble.

Fillet of a fenny snake.
In the cauldron boil and bake;
Eye of newt and toe of frog,
Wool of bat and tongue of dog. . .

Double, double toil and trouble;
Fire burn and cauldron bubble.'

'How now, you secret, black and midnight hags!' he cried. 'I conjure you, answer me!'

To his command there came a crash of thunder. From the cauldron rose a helmeted head which opened bloodless lips and spoke:

'Macbeth! Macbeth! Beware Macduff. Beware the Thane of Fife!'

The vision sank. His fears were real! Thunder rolled again, and now an infant hovered above the cauldron's stench, its body and its tiny limbs all stained with blood as though new born. It spoke!

'Be bloody, bold and resolute; laugh to scorn the power of man, for none of woman born shall harm Macbeth.'

His heart surged with new hope. 'Then live, Macduff: Why need I fear you? You had a mother who gave birth to you, as do we all . . . And yet . . . he would kill him, just to be sure, just to strangle these swarming terrors.

Thunder again: the image of a child that wore a crown and held a branch towards him.

'Be lion-mettled, proud,' the vision spoke. 'Macbeth shall never vanquished be until great Birnam Wood to high Dunsinane Hill shall come against him.'

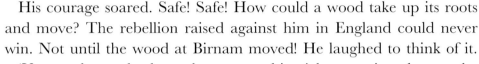

His courage soared. Safe! Safe! How could a wood take up its roots and move? The rebellion raised against him in England could never win. Not until the wood at Birnam moved! He laughed to think of it.

'Yet my heart throbs to know one thing,' he questioned urgently. 'Shall Banquo's descendants ever reign in this kingdom?'

The cauldron sank into the ground, and now there came a line of kings: one, two, three, . . . each one with Banquo's face, and the vision burned his eyes out, for their crowns shone like the sun itself . . . six, seven, and in a mirror the eighth one showed him a score of others gliding after . . . And all the while the bloody Banquo smiled and smiled and showed they were all his!

Macbeth fell to his knees, covering his face. All this vast sea of evil he had steeped his being in, and yet it would be Banquo's descendants on the throne, not his . . .

Round about the fallen figure the withered women danced.

Suddenly he was alone. He stumbled to his feet. Gone? 'Damned be all those that trust them,' he cried.

There seemed no end to Scotland's wounds. The country sank beneath the yoke of an enraged and corrupted king: it wept, it bled, and each new day a gash was added to the festering wounds. His villainies seemed to taint the very air that Scotland's people breathed.

At first, Macbeth plotted Macduff's death. But then he learned Macduff had reached England, and as if no evil was now beyond his fevered grasp, he ordered instead the deaths of all who could be found inside the castle of Macduff! The children, wife, the servants of the Thane of Fife – all put to the knife by Macbeth's murderers.

But good men began to gather against his tyranny. Macbeth went to the great castle at high Dunsinane to prepare for war, and with him went the queen.

But she was no longer like the queen. She was a shadow, pale and lifeless, except when she walked by night, asleep.

Her gentlewoman fetched the doctor to see what illness could so shake the queen that she would leave her bed and wander in the echoing halls, would make her always keep a candle by her side as though she shrank from some dark menace in the night.

They waited secretly for her. There came the flicker of her candle, and the wasted figure of the queen moved into sight. She walked as in a trance, rubbing her thin white hands as though she washed them, but with such violence as if she tried to rip the skin from every bone.

'Yet here's a spot,' she gasped. 'Out, out, damned spot! Out I say!' She shuddered: but she could see the blood was on them still!

She thought she saw her husband stand before her now, as once he was. 'Fie, my lord, fie! A soldier, and afraid! What need we fear who knows it?' She searched the dark, and sobbed, 'Who would have thought the old man to have had so much blood in him?' And she half sang, 'The Thane of Fife had a wife. Where is she now?'

Her trembling hands rose before her face.

'What, will these hands never be clean? Here's the smell of blood still.' And with a long, piteous sigh, she sobbed, 'All the perfumes of Arabia will not sweeten this little hand.'

Suddenly she stood tall and shook her head reproachfully.

'Wash your hands, put on your nightgown. Look not so pale. I tell you yet again Banquo's buried; he cannot come out of his grave.'

The listeners heard, aghast. Now the source of madness in the queen, was clear!

'Look after her,' the doctor urged. 'Remove from her the means of all harm to herself and always keep your eyes on her.'

Not far from Dunsinane the Scottish lords were gathering, and even men close to Macbeth now went to lend their strength to Malcolm's cause. They prepared to meet the English force with Malcolm and Macduff near Birnam Wood.

Macbeth fortified Dunsinane. But what need he fear these armies massing against him? Could Birnam Wood ever move to Dunsinane? 'Never! Macduff was born of woman; no man born of woman shall ever have power over me, so said the women of the heath!'

But still there was no rest for him. He reeled with tiredness and an inward, festering wound that turned all sour.

'I'll fight,' he cried, with sudden, savage rage. 'I'll fight till from my bones my flesh be hacked. Give me my armour!'

'It is not needed yet,' they told him.

'I'll put it on! Send out more horses; scour the country round; hang all those that talk of fear! Give me my armour!' And then, 'Pull it off, I say.' He flung the servant from him.

The English and the Scottish armies met at Birnam Wood. Malcolm surveyed the host of men joined with him against the tyrant and he was proud. 'Let every soldier cut down a branch and bear it before him,' he commanded. 'So shall we hide our numbers from Macbeth.'

Within the castle Macbeth gave commands. 'Hang out our banners on the outward walls.'

A sudden cry came from the inner rooms, a wail so stark, and desolate and chill it should have iced him to his heart. But what was one more desolation, one more horror to him now?

His servant brought the news.

'The queen, my lord, is dead.'

Macbeth turned away. What a vacant, futile life this was, when all was done. The future and the past yawned with arid emptiness on either side of him.

'Tomorrow and tomorrow and tomorrow creep in this petty pace from day to day to the last syllable of recorded time.' He searched for the purpose in it, but there was none. 'Life's but a tale told by an idiot, full of sound and fury, signifying nothing . . .'

A messenger burst in on him. 'As I stood watch upon the hill I looked towards Birnam and I thought the wood began to move!'

A dark, ravaging terror took Macbeth. Fear not, the fiends had said, till Birnam Wood do come to Dunsinane.

And now it came.

He thrust the terror from him. 'Arm, arm and out. Ring the alarms. Blow wind, come wrack! At least we'll die with armour on our back!'

Beyond the fortress walls the drums of Malcolm's soldiers boomed and trumpets called to war. 'Throw down your leafy screens,' Malcolm commanded his men. 'Show yourselves as those you are!'

Macbeth came from the fortress, fighting, scorning all. One final prophecy was yet to come. 'The fiends have tied me to a stake,' he cried, 'I cannot fly, but like a bear I must fight the course! What's he that was not born of woman? Such a one am I to fear, or none!'

Great Dunsinane surrendered to Malcolm's force. Now Duncan's

son and heir strode through the gates as victor of the day.

Macduff sought Macbeth everywhere. He blistered for the lives of all his murdered children, wife, and all. He burned for Scotland's wrongs.

'Turn, hell-hound, turn!' he cried.

Macbeth turned, and faced the great Macduff: traitor against royal thane. A full circle the wheel had come, since he, Macbeth, loyal thane, had faced the traitors once. It seemed as though all the evil of his poisonous days now menaced him in this one man.

'Get back,' he urged. 'My soul is weighed too heavily already with your blood. Get back!'

'I have no words, my voice is in my sword.' Macduff defied him, and leapt forward.

Macbeth held him at bay. 'I bear a charmed life,' he panted, 'which must not yield to one of woman born.'

'Then despair,' Macduff cried, 'and let the demons that have guided you tell you that I, Macduff, was ripped from my mother's womb before my time!'

So, the last twisted fruit of bitter evil was now plucked. How they had played with him, those sisters of the heath, with double talk and circling promises that lead him ever on towards false hope! And how he had fed and nurtured their poison.

But he had reached the end. And as if to redeem the broken promise of his once glorious life, he surged towards Macduff; as though by fighting he would again draw through his veins all the honour, courage and warmth that once he'd had.

But Macbeth's time was done, as was his queen's. Macduff it was that plucked his life away and drew off the poison in the land. In killing Macbeth he gave Scotland back her rightful line of kings. And with great Macbeth's death, tyranny was dead; the vicious flame of murder, treachery and disorder in the land was quenched.

Macduff bowed low before Malcolm, Prince of Cumberland. 'Hail, King of Scotland! The time is free.'

Twelfth Night

Duke Orsino
ruler of Illyria

Lady Olivia
a countess

Sir Toby Belch
a relative of Olivia

Sir Andrew Aguecheek,
Sir Toby's companion

Feste
Olivia's court jester

Maria
Olivia's maid

Malvolio
Olivia's steward

Fabian
Olivia's servant

A sea captain

Viola

Cesario
Viola in disguise

Sebastian
Viola's twin brother

Antonio
Sebastian's friend

uke Orsino was in love. Love perfumed the air with flowers, coloured the hills and cliffs with rosy light, filled the rooms in which Orsino roamed with wistful songs, their lilting notes drifting from palace balconies into the summer air.

'If music be the food of love, play on; give me excess of it,' he murmured to the strains of mournful melodies. He listened to a dying fall of notes. 'Oh, it came over my ear like the sweet sound that breathes upon a bank of violets . . .'

The duke lived for love, and dreamed of love, and sighed for love's melancholy. Indeed, if Duke Orsino's servants were to admit it (which they would not), the duke was truly in love with love itself, though he believed that the object of his adoration was a youthful and most beautiful countess named Lady Olivia.

Unfortunately for Duke Orsino, Lady Olivia did not love him. She would not love him; she could not love him; this was her only answer to his proffered love. She could love no man, for she had vowed to mourn her brother's death behind a veil, shedding tears for him in seven long years of sorrow. Since her brother's death she had allowed no visitors, no company of men near her, nor would she until the end of mourning.

And so Duke Orsino languished for love of Lady Olivia, and Lady Olivia languished for love of her dead brother, until one day, there came a stranger to that prosperous land of fair Illyria . . . Wild winds and towering waves off Illyria's rocky coast had plucked a passing ship and tossed it like a toy, spilling its passengers into the foaming waves to drift like flotsam and jetsam towards the shore.

As the storm had calmed, it threw them on the rocks, battered, drenched and exhausted by their battle with the sea, but nonetheless alive. But this was little comfort for the stranger, a young girl named Viola. Somewhere in that storm-tossed sea her twin brother, Sebastian had also been fighting for his life, and Sebastian was dearer to her than any other person in the world.

Was he dead? Or was it possible that he survived as she had? She begged the good sea captain flung ashore with her: could Sebastian be alive? The captain gave her hope: after their ship had splintered he had seen Sebastian bind himself to a mast still floating on the sea, and there he was when last the captain saw him.

'For saying so, there's gold!' Viola cried, her eyes alight with renewed hope.

But now she shivered, though the winds had softened and the air was growing warm again. What was she to do now? Here was a country she did not know, and she a woman, quite alone in it . . .

The captain saw how the young girl's fears were growing again and tried to calm them. This Illyria was a prosperous, friendly, pleasant land. He knew it well, for he had been born and bred not three hours travel from this very place. And it was ruled well by a most noble, gentle duke, Orsino.

'Orsino!' Viola said. 'I have heard my father speak of him. He was unmarried then.'

And so was he now, the captain said, though there was talk among the people that he sought the love of the lady Olivia, who mourned her brother's recent death.

Already Viola had seen a possible escape from her predicament, for though her mind was much clouded with fears for her brother's life, she had quick wits and buoyant spirits to give her strength . . . She would have liked most to serve Olivia, for it seemed that this lady might be a partner in mourning a dead brother. But the sea captain was certain she would not be accepted as a servant at Olivia's house. Olivia admitted no one.

Yet might it not be possible to obtain a position at Duke Orsino's court? Quickly she enlisted the kindly captain's help: he must lend her clothes to disguise herself as a man. She would present herself as a page at the palace of Duke Orsino of Illyria!

'I'll serve this duke!' declared Viola. 'I can sing and speak to him in many sorts of music . . .' enthusiasm for this plan began to revive her spirits and she set off with the captain, happy to have some purpose to lift her thoughts from the persistent terrors for her brother's life.

Was he dead? The thought rose again. She pushed it back. On, on, to her disguise . . . She would become Duke Orsino's page, and trust to time and hope. Only this good sea captain would know her true identity . . .

Viola's plan worked better than her wildest dreams. The grace and delicacy of her woman's shape was hidden beneath the clothes of a young man, her long fair hair tight-curled beneath a cap; and so this

pretty girl was transformed into a handsome youth whose smooth, unbearded face and light voice only made the Duke Orsino think that his new page was young, not yet having reached the age of manhood.

Viola, who in her page's disguise called herself Cesario, endeared herself to the love-sick duke with quite remarkable speed. The duke was quick to find that the 'young man' had an attentive ear and understanding eye. Within three days, 'Cesario' had heard the full history of Orsino's love for Olivia: each sigh, each loving message, each miserable rejection had been catalogued by the unhappy duke for his young page, as had the beauty, wisdom and glory of the object of his adoration, the fair Olivia.

Now Orsino asked Cesario to take up his pleas with Olivia, to be his tongue to her, and carry his messages of love.

Viola listened to the tale with a heart throbbing with more than sympathy. She watched the duke's agony of unrequited love as though it was her own. Indeed, it almost could have been, for beneath her boy's clothes, Viola, Orsino's faithful page 'Cesario', was herself suffering the pangs of unrequited love. Within three days, Viola had fallen fathoms deep in love with Duke Orsino!

And now the agony grew worse. Orsino was asking her to carry his love messages to Olivia who scorned his love – the love that she, Viola would give anything to possess! Well, she would take his messages, because of her own loyalty to the duke and (though she scarce admitted it) also because she was a little curious to find out more about Olivia.

Sir Toby Belch was as full of wind and good cheer as was his name. He was a large, rotund, jovial sort of man whose only aim in life was to consume as much food and drink as his enormous bulk could hold (preferably food and drink that others had paid for); and to do so with as much rollicking good fun, songs, games, and the exchange of wit as could be crammed into the time between getting up (recovering from being drunk), and going to bed, drunk and sated with good food.

Not content merely with his own carousing to disturb the gloom of mourning in Olivia's house, Sir Toby had seen fit to introduce another: one Sir Andrew Aguecheek, a gentleman as long and thin and pale as Sir Toby was round and plump and red. Nevertheless Sir Andrew was an excellent companion for Sir Toby, for though his brain was on the meagre side, his purse was deliciously robust and fat. More to the point, his purse was at the disposal of Sir Toby.

Sir Toby had devised a plan to keep himself in drink and food for as long as he had appetite to consume them and the strength to open his mouth. Olivia was to be persuaded to marry Sir Andrew Aguecheek. This being the general line of strategy, for the moment the tactics required that the long, thin knight should hang about the house with Sir Toby on the chance of seeing Olivia. The more Sir Andrew hung about, the more time he had to while away; the more time he had to while away, the more money he must spend; the more money he spent, the more Sir Toby made himself jovially available to share it, to keep the hopeful suitor's spirits up, to exchange a song, a dance, a joke with him . . . and generally while away the days, weeks or months . . . as chance would have it.

For a place of sombre mourning, Olivia's house indeed contained a motley collection of souls: besides the undaunted Sir Toby and the aging Andrew Aguecheek, there was also Feste, Olivia's court jester, who had a tendency to wander off on business of his own whenever the fancy took him, and who therefore also felt the sting of maid Maria's warning tongue.

'My lady will hang you for your absence!' she chided him. 'Make your excuses wisely . . . !'

And indeed, when Olivia entered, dressed head to foot in dark colours, accompanied by the sombre shadow of her steward, Malvolio, her face solemnly composed in that grieving look it had worn since her brother died, she was angry, seeing Feste.

'Take the Fool away,' she said, with a dismissive toss of her elegant head.

The Fool had quickly shaken out his wits and got them ready for fooling. He pulled his face into a mockery of her solemnity and mimicked that tossing head.

'Do you hear, fellows? Take away the lady,' he declared.

'Sir,' protested Olivia, her solemn face giving way to the temptation of a smile despite herself, 'I told them to take *you* away.'

'Give me leave,' said the Fool, catching that fleeting glimmer of mirth and determined to prise it out so that his misdemeanours would be quite forgotten by Olivia, 'Give me leave to prove *you* a fool.'

'Can you do it?' asked Olivia, curious, for she had most decidedly foresworn all merriment.

'Good madonna, why do you mourn?' enquired the Fool, with mock solemnity.

'Good Fool, for my brother's death,' said Olivia, irritated to be so unfeelingly reminded of her grief.

'I think his soul is in hell, madonna,' announced the Fool.

'I know his soul is in heaven, Fool,' retorted Olivia.

'The more fool you, madonna, to mourn for your brother's soul being in heaven. Take away the fool!'

Despite her determination not to, Olivia laughed. She turned to Malvolio, 'What do you think of this Fool, Malvolio? Does he not improve?'

Malvolio, it must be said, disapproved. What, precisely, it was that Malvolio disapproved of, would be difficult to say, for Malvolio's sharp nose was tilted in the air at everything and everyone he saw, his nostrils flared as though a most unpleasant smell was caught beneath them, his lips pressed hard together with an air of pained endurance, and his eyes half-closed as though it were pure agony to waste their light on mortals such as these . . .

'I marvel your ladyship takes delight in such a barren rascal,' he intoned with a disdainful look towards Feste. 'I saw him put down the other day with an ordinary fool that has no more brain than a stone . . .'

'Oh, you are sick of self-love, Malvolio,' Olivia interrupted him, laughing at him now. 'You taste with a sick appetite . . .'

She paused: the sound of raised voices had reached them, above all the boisterous tones of Sir Toby Belch.

Maria hurried in. There was, it seemed, a young gentleman at the gate determined to speak to Olivia.

Olivia sighed. Most probably another messenger from Orsino. She despatched Maria to rescue the messenger from Sir Toby's hospitality, for she could be fairly certain her uncle would be spouting drunken idiocies, and sent Malvolio to turn the messenger away. Any excuse would do, she was ill or not at home, anything, to rid her of this unwelcome intrusion.

It seemed, however, that not even Malvolio's disdainful nose could block the persistent young man. He was, it seemed, fortified against any denial.

Curious despite herself, Olivia enquired, 'What kind of man is he?'

'Why, of mankind,' Malvolio assured her pompously.

Olivia tried again. 'What does he look like? How old is he?'

Malvolio considered this question with some care, pursing his lips and flaring his nostrils with the effort of estimating the possible worth of such a person in Malvolio's ranks of men . . .

'Not yet old enough for a man, nor young enough for a boy,' he announced. 'As an unripe peapod before it is a . . . peapod,' he continued, 'or an unripe apple when it is almost an apple. It is, with him, like at the turn of the tide, between boy and man . . .'

Malvolio had quite lost himself in the intricacies of these poetic images . . . Olivia gave up. And then, more from boredom than anything else, she succumbed to an unexpected curiosity. She would let this messenger in, just to have a look at him.

'Give me my veil,' she told Maria. 'Throw it over my face.'

Unaware of the stir he had created in this household so firmly barred against all visitors, the stranger marched in with a stride a little too consciously masterful and a voice a little too determinedly low; for the 'he' was not a he at all; it was a she . . . It was Viola, disguised as Cesario, the love-sick duke's new page.

Faced suddenly with two unknown young women, Viola paused and stared from one to the other.

'The honourable lady of the house, which is she?' she asked.

'Speak to me; I shall answer for her,' Olivia murmured from behind the veil. But though her tone suggested she was but slightly interested, a peep behind that lacy mask would have revealed another tale. Lady Olivia, mourning or otherwise, was not immune to the charms of so handsome a young man as this 'gentleman' who stood before her now.

Viola drew a deep breath and unfolded the paper on which she had written her speech. She was determined to discharge her task for her beloved duke as faithfully as she was able.

'Most radiant, exquisite and unmatchable beauty,' she began in ringing tones, but hearing a smothered titter from Maria, she halted. She looked from Maria to the veiled lady reclining gracefully on a chair.

'I pray you, tell me if this be the lady of the house, for I never saw her,' she said to Maria. 'I would be loath to cast away my speech, for besides being excellently written, I have taken great pains to learn it.'

'Where do you come from, sir?' enquired Olivia haughtily, intrigued against her better judgement by this earnest, though somewhat cheeky, persistence.

'I can say little more than I have studied,' protested Viola. She was frustrated by her inability to get on with the task in hand and return as fast as possible to Duke Orsino's side. 'Are you the lady of the house?'

And to be truthful, she was feeling rather angry. Here was this beautiful woman supposedly in mourning, yet behaving with an unseemly coquettish tilt to her graceful head, and apparently playing games with her, while Duke Orsino languished in misery for want of love.

'Speak,' sighed Olivia, seeing now that this young man could not be turned from his declared purpose.

Viola took a deep breath and launched, 'Most sweet lady . . .'

But two more interruptions from Olivia, and Viola saw that no suit from Duke Orsino would ever penetrate this woman's heart. She stared at her in miserable disbelief. Here was a woman who had the hand and heart of Duke Orsino for the asking, yet she spurned it. What was she like, this lady made of stone?

'Good madam,' she said suddenly, growing bold, 'let me see your face.'

'Have you a mission from your lord to negotiate with my face?' Olivia enquired softly. But the request had pleased her, for this youth (or so she thought he was) absorbed her more and more with every passing minute that he stood there earnest, honest, protesting for his lord.

'But we will draw the curtain and show you the picture,' she said. Slowly, she lifted the veil and showed her exquisite face. 'Is it not well done?' she enquired, with a gleam of mockery in her dark eyes.

'Excellently done . . . if God did all,' murmured Viola, at the same time admiring the flawless beauty displayed before her, and with a woman's discerning (and perhaps a little jealous) eye, searching for the touches of artistry that might give a bloom to cheeks and lips . . .

'It will endure wind and weather,' Olivia assured her, aware only that her face had made some impression on this handsome youth, and interpreting it as the palpitations of a beating heart much like that thundering in her own breast now.

'It is true beauty,' murmured Viola, searching the face Orsino loved so passionately. She saw the arch looks and the saucy smiles being thrown towards her; her sorrow for the scorned duke and for herself, prevented by her disguise from ever seeking Orsino's love, sent a hot flush of anger to her cheeks.

'If I did love you with my master's flame, with such a suffering, such a deadly life, I would find no sense in your denial; I would not understand it,' she pleaded.

'What would you do?' Olivia whispered, her eyes fixed on the youth's face. It seemed to have grown more handsome than ever before as he spoke again of his master's love.

'I would make me a willow cabin at your gate, and call upon my soul within the house; write songs of love and sing them even in the dead of night; cry out your name to the echoing hills and make the whispers of the air murmur "Olivia"! Oh, you should not rest between the elements of air and earth, but you should pity me!'

For a long moment, Olivia sat looking at Viola's passionate face. It was as though her eyes were fastened by some magic to this youth and would never leave again.

Then she realized the look of fascination that must be showing on her face, and she dropped her eyes hurriedly, her cheeks colouring with sudden shame.

'You might do much,' she said, slowly, but she was talking to herself; for while the past half hour had started as a game, in boredom, and had continued as a tantalizing teasing of this youth, it had become now something else. Olivia was listening to echoes within her heart that she had never heard before, echoes that she had vowed she would never hear till seven long years of mourning had gone by, echoes that she had believed she could not hear, for misery at her beloved brother's death.

This youth, entering her life merely as another's messenger, seemed to carry messages of another sort which tapped these slumbering echoes . . .

She tried to gather her composure. 'Get you to your lord,' she

murmured, quietly now. 'I cannot love him; let him send no more . . .'

And then a sudden flare of daring took her again, and almost before she had realized what she said, she added hastily, 'Unless, perhaps, you come to me again . . . to tell me how he takes it. Fare you well.'

Behind the departing Viola's back, Olivia sat for a moment without moving. She could hear nothing but her thundering heart, feel nothing but the hot flush flooding her cheeks, see nothing but the vision of that handsome face ingrained for ever on her memory.

Almost before she knew what she was doing, she called Malvolio to her, pulling her ring off her finger, and holding it out to him.

'Run after that same peevish messenger, the duke's man,' she said, with a feigned air of carelessness. 'He left this ring behind.' She almost blushed at the lie, but Malvolio's nose had risen so high in the air at the sight of the disdained ring, that he was unaware of any tell-tale colours on his mistress's cheek.

'Tell him I'll have none of it,' ended Olivia hastily. 'Tell him not to flatter his lord, nor hold him up with hopes of my love; I am not for him; and,' she turned away, lest even Malvolio should see the flush rising across her face, 'if that youth will come this way tomorrow, I'll give him reasons for it.'

Nursing the ring gingerly as though it reeked of the scorned suitor, Malvolio marched out to do his mistress's will . . .

Two men were striding along a footpath that crossed a rocky headland. One, the elder, was speaking warmly, urgently, to the younger man who seemed to shake his head and plead a little with his companion . . .

To the observer who had just seen Viola dressed as Cesario march angrily from Olivia's house, the sight of what appeared to be Cesario here, high on a rocky headland on the other side of Illyria, would have caused more than a little confusion.

At closer glance, the observer might have noticed that Cesario had changed his clothes and was not wearing the finery of a duke's page, that his face was somewhat squarer, giving the appearance of being larger, and from time to time he wore a cap. (No one had ever yet seen Cesario without his cap, for the simple reason that without his cap, Cesario would have betrayed the rich tresses of a girl's fair hair.)

This Cesario had short-cropped hair, and was altogether broader, his frame much squarer . . .

And this was hardly surprising, for this was not Cesario, Viola disguised as Orsino's page. This was her brother, her twin, Sebastian whom she believed was dead, a youth so like his sister that they were almost two peas in the same pod that had so preoccupied Malvolio . . .

Shortly after his sister had safely reached the shore, Sebastian had been pulled from the waves by Antonio, the man who walked beside him now, protesting.

Their argument was simple: Antonio had grown to love this youth whose life he'd saved. He wanted Sebastian to stay.

Sebastian, on the other hand, was all for moving on. He was filled with gratitude and affection for Antonio's kindness, but he was also too well aware of how his sorrows for his sister (for he believed that she was dead) would make him always a burden to this kind man. His intention was to travel on, as fancy took him. If he stayed, tears and misery would constantly overwhelm him and he did not wish to impose his unhappiness on Antonio.

He had decided he would visit Duke Orsino's court, to see what time and fate might offer . . .

Antonio was a sea-faring man and had, in past sea-battles with Orsino's fleet, made enemies at Orsino's court: going there would be unsafe for him. Yet watching Sebastian stride away, his love for the impetuous youth was stronger than any fears for his own safety . . . He threw all care to the winds and set off to keep Sebastian company, wherever his adventures might take him.

Viola knew nothing of her brother's miraculous presence in this land. She knew only that misery seemed to grow around her by the minute. Not only was she mourning a brother's death, but she was compelled to love a man who neither loved her, nor even knew she was a woman! She was compelled to carry messages of *his* love to another woman! And this woman was as hard-hearted as she was beautiful.

Now, to crown the sorry tale, here was that same Olivia's steward pursuing her from the house, his thumb and forefinger pinched together, disdainfully holding out a ring as if it were tainted with some unmentionable disease. And now he informed her that Olivia 'returned' the ring!

'If it be worth stooping for, there it lies . . . if not, let it be his that finds it,' intoned Malvolio, opening his fingers and letting the offending jewel drop to the ground. It rolled in a circle and stopped at Viola's feet. Malvolio swung on his heel and swept away.

Viola stared at the ring. 'I left no ring with her: what does this lady mean?'

But even as Malvolio disappeared from sight an awful thought entered Viola's mind. She bent down and picked up Olivia's ring. She held it cautiously in the palm of her hand. Could this be intended as a love token? Could her appearance, her *disguised* appearance, have charmed the lady into loving her, believing her to be a man?

The appalling thought was more awful than her wildest nightmares: 'My master loves her dearly; and I love him as much; and she, mistaken, seems to dote on me!' She pondered this circle of misery with dismay. 'What will become of this?' As long as she pretended to be a man, she would remain desperate for her master's love; yet as she was truly a woman, how many purposeless sighs would poor Olivia have to breathe for love of that non-existent youth, Cesario!

'Oh, time,' sighed Viola despairingly, 'you must untangle this, not I. It is too hard a knot for me to untie.'

Sir Toby Belch was in fine form. It was long past midnight: quantities of wine and most delicious food had been consumed, and still more was to be had; and he began to thump a rhythm with his boot and tankard, while Sir Andrew Aguecheek trilled merrily after him, and Feste the jester's considerably more musical tones rounded the whole thing off into the most jovial of uproars.

The rest of the household, sensibly fast asleep, could not remain so for long. Maria was the first to appear, hastily pulling on her dressing-gown.

'What a caterwauling do you keep here!' she cried. 'If my lady has not called up her steward Malvolio and bid him turn you out of doors, never trust me!'

For answer, Sir Toby seized the irate maid by the waist and waltzed her to and fro.

'O, the twelfth day of December . . .' he carolled.

'For the love of God, peace!' pleaded Maria, half-laughing now. And then she stopped.

An apparition was at the door. A long white nightgown, crowned by a long white nightcap which in turn framed a long white face crumpled with such disdain, disgust and horror that it must surely cripple any man for life to be so burdened with it.

It was Malvolio. He halted. He surveyed the assembled company. He allowed his eyes to come to rest finally, reluctantly, on Sir Toby Belch.

'My masters, are you mad or what are you?' he enquired in a voice shrill with affronted anger. 'Have you no wit, manners, nor honesty, but to gabble like tinkers at this time of night? Is there no respect of place, persons, nor time in you?'

'We did keep time, sir, in our songs,' retorted Sir Toby, and he thumped his knee in pleasure at this last fine gem of wit.

'Sir Toby,' shrieked Malvolio in rage. 'My lady bid me tell you that, though she harbours you as her kinsman, she's not attached to your misbehaviour. If you can separate yourself and your behaviour, you are welcome to the house; if not, she is willing to bid you farewell.'

For answer Sir Toby burst forth into song, and was joined by Feste the jester, who paid no respects to any man, least of all to disgruntled household stewards who disapproved . . .

'Do you think,' Sir Toby thrust his face so close to the offended steward that Malvolio was forced to step hastily back for fear of being stifled by the fumes of ale. 'Do you think that because *you* are virtuous, there shall be no more cakes and ale?'

Malvolio had no answer. With a look of pure hatred that engulfed them all, the steward strode out, his nose higher than ever, his night cap swinging like the bell of doom, and his voice muttering darkly that Lady Olivia would hear of this . . .

Had not Maria held Sir Toby back, the infuriated man might well

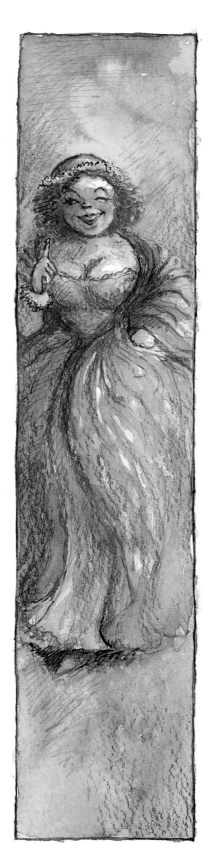

have rolled after Malvolio and boxed his ears into oblivion, for in all the rumpus Sir Toby had heard nothing of Olivia's pleas for good behaviour in her house; he heard only the insolent, offensive, always disapproving tones of Malvolio, whose gloomy face and appalling vanity seemed to bring the only cloud on to Sir Toby's jovial horizon, but a cloud that was always there.

'Sweet Sir Toby, be patient for tonight,' urged Maria. She had come herself in irritation at the noise made by Sir Toby and his fellow revellers; but in an instant this had been transformed by Malvolio's sour face into a burning desire to teach the acid-tongued steward a lesson, to find some sweet revenge . . .

'Since the youth of the duke was with my lady, she is much disturbed,' she warned Sir Toby Belch. 'As for Monsieur Malvolio, leave him to me . . .'

Sir Toby saw that some plan was taking shape in her sharp brain. In gleeful anticipation, he wrapped his arms about her robust waist, and planted an exuberant kiss on both her cheeks.

With a laughing tap on his nose, Maria swung herself free, and clapped her hands for their attention. The plan was in her mind, perfect . . . 'I will drop in his way some obscure letters of love,' she told her attentive audience, 'where, by the colour of his beard, the shape of his leg, the manner of his walk, the expression of his eyes, forehead and complexion, he shall find himself most accurately described. I can write very like my lady, your niece . . .'

'Excellent! I smell a trick!' Sir Toby slapped his knee in pure delight.

'I have it in my nose too!' chortled Sir Andrew Aguecheek . . .

'And he shall think,' Toby's brain was far from slow, and in that instant he had seen Maria's brilliant device, 'he shall think, by the letters you will drop, that they come from my niece and that she's in love with him!' He bellowed in ecstasy at the thought of any temptation to Malvolio's disgusting vanity.

'I will hide you two where he shall find the letter,' Maria assured them. 'Observe what he makes of it!' She wagged her finger at the drunken pair. 'For this night, to bed, and dream on the event!'

'Come, come, I'll go drink some sherry; it is too late to go to bed now,' declared Sir Toby. He wrapped his arm around the swaying Sir Andrew's shoulders. 'Come, knight! Come, knight!'

Duke Orsino was talking of love. 'If ever you love, in the sweet pangs of it, remember me,' he told 'Cesario', whose attentive ear provided him with greater comfort than he had ever had. Once more he had been rejected by Olivia. Once more he languished in the misery of unrequited love.

Orsino looked searchingly at Viola, though he saw no more than the figure of his faithful page Cesario and not the face of a woman who adored him more with every minute that she spent by his side. 'Young though you are, your eye has strayed upon some person that it loves, has it not, boy?' he enquired, gently and with a fatherly expression in his eyes.

'A little,' admitted Viola.

'What kind of woman is it?' the duke enquired.

'Of your complexion,' Viola replied, with beating heart.

'She is not worth you, then,' the duke dismissed this. 'And how old?'

'About your age, my lord,' Viola whispered, and looked with scarcely disguised longing into his face . . .

Orsino, of course, did not see that tell-tale lustre in her eyes. His thoughts had moved again to Olivia, and poor Viola was once more to be no more than his messenger to that lady, carrying further words of Orsino's undying love.

'But if she cannot love you, sir,' Viola protested, frustrated with this thankless task and distressed that she would be again the bearer of such hurtful news to this man that she adored.

'I cannot accept that answer,' Orsino pushed the thought away.

'But you must!' persisted Viola. 'Say that some lady, as perhaps there is,' she wondered if the flush colouring her cheeks could be seen by Duke Orsino, 'say that some lady has for your love as great a pang of heart as you have for Olivia: you cannot love her; you tell her so; must she not then be answered?'

'There is no woman's heart can hold the beating of so strong a passion as love gives to my heart,' cried the heart-sick duke. 'Make no comparison between the love a woman can bear me and that I owe Olivia!'

'Aye, but I know . . .' Viola burst out, in misery.

'What do you know?' enquired the duke.

Viola was so close to spilling out her love for him, that in a moment she would have plunged across the precipice. 'Too well what love women may bear for men,' she cried. 'My father had a daughter loved

a man, as might be . . . perhaps, . . . were I a woman . . . I should love your lordship . . .'

The duke looked at his earnest page with some amusement. He put an arm about the young lad's shoulders, 'And what's her history?'

Viola lowered her eyes, afraid that he would see the light of love in them. 'A blank, my lord,' she murmured. 'She never told her love, but let concealment, like a worm in the bud, feed on her damask cheek: she pined in thought, and with a green and yellow melancholy she sat like patience on a monument, smiling at grief . . .'

And she smiled up at him, mistress of her unruly emotions once again. 'Was this not love indeed?'

'But did your sister die of her love, my boy?' the duke persisted, intrigued by this melancholy tale.

'I am all the daughters of my father's house . . .' whispered Viola almost lost again, and teetering on the brink of telling all . . . 'and all the brothers too . . .' she ended hastily. She turned from him, quickly composing her face as was more fitting for the servant of a noble duke. 'Sir, shall I to this lady?'

'Aye, that's the theme. To her in haste,' Orsino urged. 'Give her this jewel, say my love can give no place, waits no denial . . .'

The letter glinted, tantalizing in the morning sun. Behind the exuberant blooms of a large flowering bush, three figures crouched, though there could be nothing secret about their presence there. Sir Toby chortled, Sir Andrew cackled, and Fabian, another of Olivia's servants, hissed and hushed at them both. To any other person walking in that sunlit garden, the dishevelled, boisterous trio would have been instantly visible.

But not to Malvolio. Malvolio was busy. Malvolio was deep in a most exquisite fantasy. Malvolio was not Malvolio, Olivia's servant, but Malvolio, a great and powerful nobleman . . . and Malvolio had been practising a nobleman's behaviour to his own shadow for the past half hour. Indeed Malvolio was quite lost in this inspiring vision of himself. He addressed the trees, the sky, the sun, and all were courtiers to him . . .

'To be Count Malvolio,' he said, rolling the words around his tongue, 'having been three months married to Olivia . . . calling my officers about me,' he waved a peremptory hand towards the trees, 'in my branched velvet gown, having come from a day-bed where I have left Olivia sleeping . . .'

'Fire and brimstone!' spluttered Sir Toby Belch, and nearly fell out of the bush. He was yanked back out of sight by Fabian.

'Telling them . . .' Malvolio smirked at the thought of this next vision, 'telling them, I know my place as I wish them to know theirs . . . to ask for my kinsman, Toby . . .'

'Belts and shackles!' this time Sir Toby exploded from the bush, and had to be hauled back by the combined strengths of Fabian and Sir Andrew . . .

Malvolio's fantasy continued. 'I frown the while,' the sky was withered by his frown, 'perchance wind up my watch or play with . . . some rich jewel; Toby approaches; curtsies there to me . . .' Malvolio's face took on an air of pained dignity. He held a hand out to the imaginary Toby. 'I extend my hand to him thus, quenching my familiar smile with an austere regard of control . . .'

'And does not Toby give you a blow on the lips then?' shrieked Toby, muzzled instantly by Fabian, who was determined to see out this escapade, for he too had fallen foul of Malvolio's pinch-faced disapproval and felt that a ripe punishment for such a man would be a good day's work.

But now Malvolio's prancing feet had neared the letter that lay in wait for him. It was Maria's letter, faking the handwriting of Olivia, and laid carefully on the path for him to find . . .

'By my life, this is my lady's writing!' exclaimed Malvolio on cue. He unfolded the paper, carefully, and paying little attention to the possibility that such a letter might be private to her ladyship, began to read. 'Jove knows I love: but who? Lips do not move; no man must know,' he read the tantalizing words aloud. And then a thought struck him. Transfixed, he stood there, clasping the letter to his chest, his face suddenly aflame with knowledge. If these words should be for him!

The watchers tittered. Could the man truly be so easily caught? A riddle, a few clues (some of the letters of Malvolio's name, which his brain deciphered slowly), and Maria's trap was set: Malvolio was utterly convinced the letter was from Olivia, writing in secret, to him.

He read on. 'If this fall into your hands, revolve.' Malvolio spun on his heels. 'In my stars I am above you.' He looked up. And then he understood the clue and drew a deep breath of pure, glorious satisfaction. Of course! *Lady* Olivia was of noble birth, and so above him. He

returned with rapt attention to the letter: 'but be not afraid of greatness,' it went on. 'Some are born great, some achieve greatness, and some have greatness thrust upon them . . . Remember who commended your yellow stockings, and wished to see you always cross-gartered . . . If you return my love, let it appear in your smiling; your smiles become you well; therefore in my presence smile, dear my sweet, I beg you . . .'

Malvolio stood in silence, gazing at the glorious letter. Then he clasped it to his bosom. He raised his eyes to heaven. 'I will smile!' he cried, 'I will do everything that you wish!' and in a paroxysm of delight he rushed away, to clad himself in the yellow stockings and cross-garters, and to prepare the smile that would eclipse all smiles, for Olivia . . .

Unable to control their mirth any longer, Sir Toby, Fabian and Sir Andrew fell out of the bush, and rolled across the path, stopping only when Maria appeared, eager to know if her letter had achieved the desired effect.

'Why, you have put him in such a dream,' gasped Sir Toby Belch, 'that when the image of it leaves him he must run mad!'

'If you will then see the fruits of this sport,' Maria interrupted her fellow plotters' raucous laughter, 'mark his first approach before my lady: he will come to her in yellow stockings, and . . .' she snorted with laughter, 'it is a colour she loathes; and cross-gartered, a fashion she detests; and he will smile upon her, which will now be so unsuitable to her mood . . . !'

Viola's discomfort was growing by the minute. Once more forced to visit Olivia on behalf of Duke Orsino, she must endure not merely her master's rejection, but now an open wooing of herself! Olivia, by turns made shy or bold as the throbs of love filled her with courage or plunged her into abject shame, now declared her love for Orsino's page!

'Cesario, by the roses of the spring, by maidhood, honour, truth and everything, I love you so!' she cried. 'In spite of all your pride, neither wit nor reason can hide my passion.'

'By innocence I swear, and by my youth, I have one heart, one bosom and one truth, and that no woman has,' Viola cried. What was she to do in this extraordinary predicament? Such ardent sighs from Lady Olivia! Such gleaming eyes! Such longing hand-clasps, from which Viola escaped only with difficulty. 'Nor shall anyone be mistress of my heart except I alone,' she protested frantically. 'And so, farewell, good madam!'

This must, she promised herself, be absolutely the last visit to the countess for her master. She could endure this miserable confusion for not a minute more!

Sir Andrew Aguecheek was most unhappy. He had seen the countess pay more attention in a few moments to the duke's new page than she had paid in *weeks* to hopeful Andrew Aguecheek.

And with this he had finally seen enough. He would not stay a moment longer!

Sir Toby was made suddenly aware that the fat purse that lined their days with comforts was about to be whisked beyond his reach. Instantly, Sir Toby and Fabian were awash with words of hearty encouragement: the problem (as they put it to the disappointed knight) was that Olivia was watching to see how Sir Andrew would perform against this upstart page. The answer to the problem lay simply in challenging Cesario to a duel. Would not such a duel be closely watched by Lady Olivia? Was she not plainly eager to know how her favoured suitor, good Sir Andrew, would fare!

So was the pouting Sir Andrew transformed again. He set off, much cheered, to write his challenge to the page who dared to try to claim Olivia's heart from him!

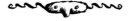

Sebastian and Antonio had at last arrived in town. Antonio, concerned not to be seen by any who would recognize him, had gone straight to find them lodgings in the suburbs and arranged to meet Sebastian there later. Sebastian set off to wander curiously around the town, to look at the sights for which the place was famed, and do a little shopping with the money which good Antonio had left him for his use, stowed safely in Antonio's own purse.

Meanwhile Olivia had sent for Cesario again. She waited nervously
for the arrival of this youth, for she was by now so deeply in love with
him that her whole existence seemed to hang on her adoration of him.
She had forgotten what it was once like not to know him or to love
him.

She waited, pacing before the door, wringing her hands, straightening
her hair, her skirt . . . how exactly should she behave towards Cesario?
What could she do to win his love?

For her pains, she got not Cesario, but Malvolio. And what a Malvolio!
Brilliant in sunshine-yellow stockings, like some gigantic stalking bird,
his legs laced most exotically with intricate cross-gartering, a smile
from ear to ear like an enormous wound from which his teeth
loomed, glistening . . . and such a wealth of knowing nods
and winks, and kissing hands towards Olivia . . .

Olivia drew back in horror, quite unprepared for this
transformation of her sober steward. Was this the man
she relied on utterly to maintain the calm and
smooth-running of a sombre house of mourning?
The poor man must be dreadfully ill!

And there he was, leering and winking
again, while all the while the strangest of
words dropped from his ever-smiling mouth . . .

'Be not afraid of greatness!' he grinned
grotesquely at Olivia and twirled a shapely
yellow-gartered leg; 'it was well written,' he
assured her. 'Some are born great, some achieve
greatness . . .' he pranced before her, his smile stretching
till it seemed to split his face in two. Then, with a string
of wild flourishes with one flapping hand, he bent low
before Olivia, to grimace ludicrously into her startled face,
'and some have greatness thrust upon them!' he finished,
with a knowing wink.

Olivia, of course, knew nothing of the fake letter which had provided
Malvolio's guide for this inspired performance. These antics from her
usually impeccable steward were beyond her comprehension. There
was no explanation for it but that the poor, blighted man had
gone quite mad. With news of Cesario's arrival distracting her,
she hastily gave orders that Malvolio should be taken care of,
for she would not have harm come to him for all the world . . .

So it was that Sir Toby came to be entrusted with the care of 'mad' Malvolio! What a perfect place from which to exact revenge . . . and what a revenge it proved to be!

If Malvolio was behaving in a fashion for which the only explanation was his madness, why then mad he would be called, and with what gusto did Sir Toby, Sir Andrew, Fabian and Feste enter into this scheme of Malvolio's madness. Malvolio could not open his mouth, but that his audience squealed at the poor man's confusion of wit, he could not utter a single sound, but that they berated the 'foul fiends and devils' which had taken possession of his soul . . . And the more they baited Malvolio, the angrier, ruder, and more arrogant the man became, for had not the letter also said he should deal roughly with servants, rudely with kinsman . . . ?

It all fitted so perfectly with Malvolio's expectations, and the letter had stroked his vanity with such audacity, that he followed, nose up in the air, right into the trap without a suspicion in the world that this was anything other than the device by which his mistress wished to show her secret love for him and urge him to show his love for her!

Sir Toby in revenge was ruthless. In a trice he had confined his victim in a pitch-dark room, bound hand and foot for being a madman, there to endure his plight until such time as Toby might feel pity for the man . . .

Meanwhile Sir Toby's main concern was to keep Sir Andrew and his purse firmly in Olivia's house.

That hopeful knight had valiantly struggled off to write a challenge to 'Cesario'. He returned with some writing which was as addled as his meagre brain. This prize he entrusted proudly to Sir Toby, to be conveyed with all due ceremony to Cesario.

Behind his back, Sir Toby and Fabian were quick to hide what Sir Andrew had written. If Cesario should read this missive from the 'challenger', he could not help but see the towering heights of idiocy, not bravery, that spurred on the aged knight who dared him to a duel.

Instead, Sir Toby waylaid Cesario and most eloquently conveyed Sir Andrew's challenge by word of mouth. So vivid was the report of Sir Andrew Aguecheek's bravery and skill, his fury, deadly speed and daring, that it would have sent any youth into a state of nervousness over the safety of his life. It sent Cesario into a state of abject terror, for Viola had never even held a weapon in her hand and possessed neither the slightest skill, nor any will to fight. The prospect of duels, blood and death merely curdled her brain, transformed her strong straight legs into trembling pins that buckled at the knees, her arms into quivering rubber that had no strength even to hold the offending sword, and her voice, which she normally succeeded in pitching low enough to have some semblance of a young man's tones, to a pitiful squeak . . . the more so because the poor girl did not have the faintest idea what should have caused such anger against her.

All her efforts to escape the duel only caught her faster in the trap: according to Sir Toby Belch, a knight like fierce Sir Andrew Aguecheek would let no one rest until his challenge had been answered . . .

Returning as swiftly as his bloated bulk allowed, Sir Toby filled Sir Andrew's reeling head with terrors of a similar sort. This page of Duke Orsino's was a very devil! Such a skill with swords! There was no peace to be made with such a man: nothing but a duel to the death would satisfy him!

Sir Andrew swayed and would have fainted, but Sir Toby marched the wilting knight towards his doom . . .

His doom, in the shape of Viola praying that the ground would open up and swallow her, grew deathly pale. She beheld this bringer of destruction march towards her, and saw he was held back from his thirst for blood only by the sheer strength of his two companions! She trembled, and clutched at the sword Toby had thrust into her hands . . .

'Put up your sword!' the fierce cry seemed to come from nowhere, and like a thunderbolt from heaven, a man leapt out in front of her, his broad shape blocking off the waving sword of Andrew Aguecheek. 'If this young gentleman has done offence, I take the fault on me,' he shouted at the knight. 'If you offend *him*, I defy you for him!' and standing belligerently before Viola, the stranger held his own weapon menacingly, daring anyone to move towards her . . .

The speed with which her fate had been transformed from certain death to daring rescue by a total stranger was too much for Viola. Relief and shock flooded over her and turned her legs to water . . .

Who was this man? She had never seen him before, nor the soldiers who burst in and set upon her saviour, and had him bound between two stout guards before she had even recovered from the last shock. Arrested! By Duke Orsino's men!

And there was more. Now this stranger turned a look of love on her, and in a gruff, gentle voice, spoke as though he knew her!

'This comes with seeking you,' Antonio said, for Viola's rescuer was none other than this loyal friend of her own brother, Sebastian. And Antonio looked with sorrow on the youth that he had just rescued, whom he believed was Sebastian. 'But my necessity makes me ask you for my purse . . .'

Purse? She had no purse of his! Viola began to wonder now if she was going mad.

Antonio halted, having seen her look of blank denial. He searched her face. A look of disbelieving horror crept across it. Denied! Thrown off when most he needed help! He tried again. 'I must ask you for some of that money.'

'What money, sir?' Viola asked in all innocence. 'For the fair kindness you have showed me here, I'll lend you something!'

He appealed in desperation to the soldiers who still held him fast. 'This youth that you see here I snatched one half out of the jaws of death . . . But oh how vile an idol is this god! Sebastian . . . !'

Sebastian! Viola's mind could barely hold the word. This man mistook her for another called Sebastian! A surge of thoughts rushed through her head: her own brother Sebastian looked very much like she did . . . even his clothes would be a little like the ones she wore, for it was Sebastian's style that she had followed in making up her page's clothes . . .

Could this stranger's Sebastian be her own brother? Could brother Sebastian be, after all these months, alive?

Sebastian, ignorant of the grim fate that had befallen his good friend Antonio, and still wandering idly about the town, filled up his time with small activities to erase the misery that filled his heart at memories of his sister's death.

Imagine then his irritation when he was accosted by a cheeky jester who claimed to know him well, and claimed he had been sent to find him by his mistress!

'Go to, you are a foolish fellow,' Sebastian retorted. 'Let me be rid of you.'

'No, I do not know you,' Feste mocked, for it was he. 'Nor am I sent to you by my lady to bid you come and speak with her; nor your name is not Master Cesario; nor this is not my nose, neither. Nothing that is so is so!'

'I beg you, vent your folly somewhere else. You do not know me,' Sebastian dismissed him.

But hardly had he turned from this than he was set upon by a great beanpole of a gentleman who waved a sword as though it were a wand and stabbed the air with it, egged on by a monstrous, bloated wine-barrel of a man . . .

'Are all the people mad?' Sebastian yelled, drawing his sword to defend himself, and dealing the prancing knight a solid, no-nonsense blow.

Sir Andrew, who had been hit in the arm, and Sir Toby who had been hit nowhere but in his expectations that they were going to thrash their victim soundly, . . . stared in some confusion at the youth they thought was young Cesario. What, quaking at the knees a moment ago when the soldiers came, and now no less than a raging tiger of a man! Incensed, Sir Toby grabbed Sir Andrew's sword . . .

'Hold, Toby; on your life, I charge you, hold!' Olivia's furious voice rang out and stopped even Sir Toby in his bull-like rush towards his quarry.

'Ungracious wretch,' she hurled at him. 'Out of my sight!' Then she turned with such a glow of love towards Sebastian. 'Be not offended, dear Cesario,' she calmed him, and her tones were golden honey with the warmth of adoration in them.

Sebastian stood rooted to the ground in wonderment, disbelief and awe (tinged with an adventurer's lightning flash of insight at his miraculous good fortune). Apparently there was one Cesario much sought after in these parts, and much beloved by this jewel of a lady! Apparently he, Sebastian, was being mistaken for this Cesario. So either *they* were mad, or *he* was mad, or else this was a dream; and if it was a dream, why then, let him sleep on . . .

While all the world ran circles round Sebastian, believing him to be Cesario, and Antonio was arrested defending Cesario, believing him to be Sebastian, Malvolio was still shut away and treated as a madman by Sir Toby and his accomplices.

Now they persuaded Feste to dress up in a gown and beard and go to him: adopting a priest's solemn, sing-song tones, Feste duly hailed Malvolio through the tiny window of his dismal prison.

From inside there came the startled cry 'Who calls there?'

'Sir Topas the priest, who comes to visit Malvolio the lunatic,' intoned Feste the jester.

'Sir Topas, Sir Topas, good Sir Topas, go to my lady,' pleaded Malvolio, the hood-winked steward. 'Never was a man thus wronged: good Sir Topas do not think me mad: they have laid me here in hideous darkness!' and at this last the poor man's voice quite broke with the horror and the terror of his plight.

Listening, even Sir Toby felt a twinge of some regret, though it was less for Malvolio's plight than for his own.

'Go to him in your own voice,' he urged Feste, 'bring me word how you find him. I wish we were well rid of this joke. If he could be conveniently released, I wish he were, for I am now so far out of favour with my niece that I cannot go any further with this sport . . .'

The familiar tones of Feste the jester reached Malvolio in his darkened cell and new hope surged through his black despair.

'Good fool,' he begged the jester with a respect he had never used before to him, 'Good fool, help me to a candle, pen, ink and paper: as I am a gentleman, I will live to be thankful to you for it.'

'Master Malvolio?' Feste enquired, with mock surprise.

'They keep me in darkness and do all they can to keep me out of my wits,' Malvolio cried. 'Good fool, help me to some light and some paper,' he repeated his pitiful refrain. 'I tell you, I am as well in my wits as any man in Illyria . . .'

On the question of how mad or sane were the people of Illyria, Sebastian at least would have been hard put to give a clear reply. Here was he, snatched from the jaws of death, plunged deep in sorrow for his sister's death, transported suddenly into a world of glory where the most exquisite lady (a countess, no less, and wealthy, too) adored him . . .

'This is the air; that is the glorious sun,' he told himself. 'This pearl she gave me, I do feel it and see it; and though it is wonder that surrounds me, yet it is not madness.' But then again, could he be certain of that?

And where was Antonio? His disappearance was bewildering. Sebastian had looked in vain for him at their arranged meeting place. Antonio had indeed been there, and had after scoured the town searching for Sebastian. But since, the man had disappeared!

And even as he pondered this strangest of strange accidents which brought him into the arms of this exquisite lady, Olivia herself appeared. She brought a priest with her, and now she begged Cesario (for so she believed Sebastian to be), to vow before the priest that he would marry her!

She stared breathlessly at Sebastian, in that instant suddenly appalled at her own audacity . . .

'What do you say?' she whispered, hardly daring to hear Cesario's answer. How little time had passed since she pursued Cesario with little encouragement to love, and yet how swiftly his cool rejection had become an ardent passion . . .

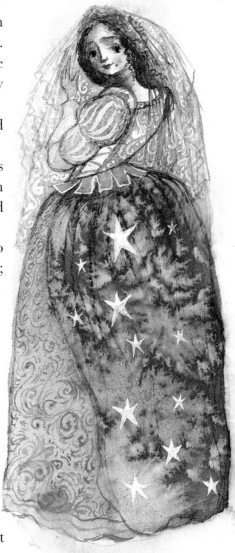

Now, waiting nervously for his reply, her fears were swiftly put to rest. 'Cesario' clasped her to his heart, and answered, 'I'll go with you; and having sworn truth, ever will be true.'

The Duke Orsino could stand no more rejection from Olivia. For months he had sung of his love by letter, messenger, gifts, poems, and nothing had won her heart. Now he came himself.

And Viola came too, nervous for her lord and for herself . . . she dared not think what might happen next!

What was to become of this appalling tangle of events? Orsino loved a woman, who loved Orsino's page, who was a woman hiding as a man, who loved Orsino . . .

They got no further than Olivia's garden.

'Here comes the man, sir, that rescued me!' Viola cried, relieved that she could show her saviour to the duke, for he alone could release Antonio from his guards.

The duke eyed the man slowly. 'That face I do remember well, yet when I saw it last, it was besmeared in the smoke of war . . .' he told Viola. 'He was the captain of a vessel that grappled with the most noble ship of our fleet . . .'

'He did me kindness, sir, drew his weapon in my defence, though in doing so he spoke so strangely . . .'

Antonio had been standing there, his dark eyes fixed in smouldering defiance on Viola. This final betrayal was too much for him. 'Orsino, noble sir,' he burst out, 'that most ungrateful boy there by your side . . .' in a fury of hurt he poured out his tale: how he had snatched the youth from raging seas, had brought him back to life and grown to love him . . . how he had thrown all care to the winds to follow him, protect him, care for him . . . for which he had received only betrayal, denial, and the crowning insult . . . 'he even denied me my own purse which I gave him for his use not half an hour before!'

'When did he come to this town?' Orsino asked, intrigued, for clearly the man spoke with an honest belief in the truth of his own tale.

'Today, my lord,' Antonio replied, 'and for three months before, both day and night, we did keep company.'

'Fellow, your words are madness,' the duke assured him, 'for three months this youth has waited upon me . . .' but even this engaging mystery was put to sudden flight from Orsino's mind, for Olivia had entered the room, and Orsino had no eyes for anyone else.

Olivia, however, had no eyes for any but Cesario.

Though she was courteous enough in greeting to the duke, her gaze was fastened only on his page.

'Cesario, you do not keep promise with me,' she challenged, with a look of hurt.

The duke heard this at first with incomprehension. But having once again tried to gain Olivia's attention and found it was locked fast on young Cesario, a new thought entered the rejected lover's brain. It was Cesario the lady loved! This final rejection was more than he could stand; he could be as cruel as she! He would take away this youth that she adored, to spite her love . . .

Now Olivia saw her passionate lover of a few hours ago, willingly prepared to go off with the duke!

'Where does Cesario go?' she cried.

'After him I love more than I love these eyes, more than my life, more than ever I shall love a wife,' Viola declared, throwing all caution off, and turning ardently towards her lord.

Orsino looked at her in some surprise. This passion, though he knew the youth was fond of him, was not expected. Viola, feeling her loved one's searching eyes on her, raised hers and met his gaze, then in confusion flushed deep red . . .

'Cesario, husband, stay,' shrieked Olivia.

'Husband!' yelled the duke. Betrayed by his page!

This appalling truth was instantly confirmed by the priest who had married them not two hours before!

Viola heard this information with horror no less than that which filled the duke. She stared from Olivia to Orsino, whose look of rage and hurt almost wilted her. That he should think she would betray him thus; that Olivia could believe she would betray him thus . . . !

Olivia, for her part, looked from Orsino to Viola in panic. Where was the eager lover of two hours ago, the man who had leapt to her love with the heat of passion that matched her own?

While all the while Antonio looked on, scowling at Viola, as did Orsino, as did Olivia, each believing this youth to be a master of betrayal, a man without a soul, heart or honour of any kind . . .

Into this bewildered circle stumbled Sir Andrew with bleeding head, followed by Toby Belch, clutching his head and moaning, fleeing (so they said) from the duke's young gentleman, Cesario, who had viciously set upon them but a moment ago . . .

And there he stood! Even Sir Toby now shrank a little from the sight of him . . .

Everyone stared at Viola. A liar, a betrayer, and now a breaker of men's heads!

And a man who could by magic split himself in two! For suddenly a second Cesario sprang before their astounded eyes. 'I am sorry, madam, I have hurt your kinsman,' he cried out to Lady Olivia. 'Pardon me, sweet one, even for the vows we made each other, so little time ago!'

There was a silence. Olivia stared from the Cesario who now acknowledged his vows to her to the Cesario who denied them. Viola gazed with fast-beating heart upon this mirror-image of herself and scarcely dared to hope . . .

The duke whispered, 'One face, one voice and two persons!' While Sebastian, for the newcomer was he, spotted Antonio and rushed towards him with his hands outstretched, 'Antonio, oh my dear Antonio! How have the hours racked and tortured me since I have lost you!'

'Sebastian, are you he?' said Antonio, suspiciously, for the misery of these past hours had wiped away his trust of any man. 'How have you made division of yourself? An apple, sliced in two, is not more twin than these two creatures! Which is Sebastian?'

For the first time, Sebastian became aware of his other self. He gaped at the apparition: what new madness in this land of madness was this trick? He laughed, for perhaps the trick would laugh itself away. But still it stood there, and still the duke, Olivia, and Antonio stood looking at them both, from one to the other and back again.

'I never had a brother. Nor can I be here and everywhere!' Sebastian assured them, though by now he was beginning to wonder if he could say even this with any certainty. 'But I had a sister . . .' and even as he said this, a new hope began to stir in him . . .

Viola took a step towards him. 'Sebastian was my father; such a Sebastian was my brother, too . . .' for in that moment she, at least, had understood . . .

'Were you a woman,' cried Sebastian, 'I would let my tears fall upon your cheek, and say, "welcome, drowned Viola!" '

With a sweep Viola tore the cap from her head and let her long hair tumble down. 'My father had a mole upon his brow!' she cried.

'And so had mine,' yelled Sebastian.

'And died that day Viola turned thirteen!' Viola shrieked, and fell upon her brother's neck in tears of joy.

And so the tangle was untied, and all explained, forgiven, and repaired. Olivia, who had unwittingly loved a girl and believed herself betrayed, now found herself united, as she longed for, with a man. Viola, whose sorrow for her brother's death had remained with her for three long months, was now miraculously clasped in his living arms. And the duke . . .

The duke had watched these moments of revelation and discovery with fascination. As the truth began to dawn on him, so was his heart and mind awash with sudden memories of all the months in which his devoted page had offered him companionship, and sympathy . . . and love . . .

He turned now to gaze at Viola with an eye and heart uncluttered by his worship of Olivia. He looked at Viola not as a gentle youth to whom he gave his confidence, but as a woman, and in that instant, knew he loved her as he had never loved Olivia. He loved her as a person that he knew and understood and truly cared for, not an idol that he painted in his mind in colours that were not her own . . .

And he remembered her own words to him. 'Boy,' he said, with a teasing mockery in his eyes, 'you have said to me a thousand times that you never would love any woman as you loved me . . .'

'And all those sayings will I swear again,' Viola said, throwing all caution to the winds, 'and all those swearings keep as true in soul as is the sun that keeps the day from night . . .'

'Give me your hand, and let me see you in your woman's clothes,' Orsino cried.

And so two pairs of tangled lovers were untangled, and retied with the one they loved: Sebastian to Olivia and Orsino to Viola.

But two others languished still alone: Antonio knew that he had lost the companionship of the young man he adored; but yet there was a compensation in the knowledge that no betrayal of his trust had taken place.

And Malvolio? What of Malvolio, poor hood-winked Malvolio, whose fantasy of love had led him to a trap beyond his wildest nightmares?

Followed closely by Malvolio, Feste the jester, true to his word, now delivered a letter from that poor despairing man to Olivia . . .

And so it came about that Maria's letter, faking Olivia's handwriting was produced. In a moment the plot was laid before Olivia, Malvolio's plight revealed in all its misery, as was the role of Toby, Fabian and Maria and the jester, to say nothing of Sir Andrew Aguecheek . . .

Though these admissions were not given without a full and vivid catalogue of those injuries at Malvolio's hand that had prompted them all to take revenge . . .

'Alas, how they have baffled you,' sighed Olivia to Malvolio.

'And thus the whirligig of time brings in his revenges,' Feste chanted.

'I'll be revenged on the whole pack of you,' declared Malvolio, his nose returning to its customary height above the ground, his mouth to its customary pinched pout, whirling on his heel with his customary snort, to march away from them.

'He has been notoriously abused,' said Olivia, watching the offended man disappear from sight with sorrow.

'Pursue him,' urged Orsino, for whom no cloud would mar this day of unexpected happiness. 'Entreat him to a peace.' And now he turned with joy towards his faithful page.

'Cesario, come, for so you shall be, while you are a man; but when in other garments you are seen, Orsino's mistress, and his fancy's queen!'

And now the garden of this stately home in fair Illyria was emptied of its lovers gained and lovers lost. Only the jester Feste stayed, to linger in the fading sunshine, and to sing a little, mournful song . . .

> 'When that I was and a little tiny boy,
> With a hey, ho, the wind and the rain,
> A foolish thing was but a toy,
> For the rain it raineth every day . . .'

A Midsummer Night's Dream

Duke Theseus
ruler of Athens

Hippolyta
his bride-to-be

Hermia

Hermia's father

Lysander

Demetrius

Helena

THE WORKMEN

Peter Quince
the carpenter

Francis Flute
the bellows mender

Tom Snout
the tinker

Robin Starveling
the tailor

Snug
the joiner

Nick Bottom
the weaver

THE FAIRIES

Oberon
King of Fairies

Puck
*a goblin
servant to Oberon*

Titania
Queen of Fairies

Titania's fairies

How slow the old moon waned! Four days until the bright new moon brought in the wedding day of great Duke Theseus. Four days to watch the old moon lingering and dream of pleasures yet to come. But with what triumph, pomp and celebration then would Theseus marry fair Hippolyta beneath the new moon's silver bow: though he had wooed and won her with the sword, now he would wed this Queen of Amazons with mirth and merriment and revelling through all of Athens.

There were others who watched the passage of the waning moon with anxious eyes. There was a girl of Athens named Hermia, whose father wanted her to wed Demetrius, a rich and handsome youth most suitable as a husband. But Hermia did not love Demetrius. She loved Lysander, also rich and handsome, but to young Hermia's eyes so much finer than any other youth. Lysander had won her heart with poetry, by moonlight sung of love, showered her with tokens of his adoration, flowers, rings and locks of hair . . .

The father stormed against his daughter, who with her passionate tongue and stubborn disobedience, refused Demetrius and declared her love for young Lysander. He came in anger to Duke Theseus to demand the law against his rebellious child. Either she should marry the man he chose, or suffer the punishment decreed by law: death, or live out her days far from the company of men, locked in a nunnery.

Duke Theseus gave Hermia until the next new moon, his wedding day, to make her choice. On that day she must declare herself: either to marry Demetrius, as her father wished, or let the laws of Athens take their course.

The lovers would not yield. To be forced to choose their love through others' eyes! Rather, they would flee the laws of Athens, and marry without a father's or a duke's consent!

So they agreed, and in a wood outside the walls of Athens they arranged to meet, the following night, by moonlight . . .

Demetrius, though fiercely scorned by Hermia, yet loved her passionately. But he was adored by another girl of Athens: Helena. Helena was Hermia's closest friend: since childhood they had played and shared together.

But now Helena, who loved Demetrius with all her body and soul, found that he merely spurned her passionate devotion, and emptied all his love on her *friend* Hermia! He had eyes only for Hermia's dark eyes, ears only for Hermia's rich voice. The more *Hermia* frowned on him, the more he loved her! The more *Hermia* showed her hate, the more he followed her.

While she, poor loving Helena, found only that the more she followed Demetrius, the more he hated her!

There was no sense or fairness in love's choices! Hermia was small and strong and dark with deep brown eyes and raven hair. Helena was tall and slim and fair with soft blue eyes. Many in Athens (as Helena told herself) considered her no less beautiful than Hermia, and before Demetrius had loved Hermia, he had poured out vows of love to *Helena*. When he saw Hermia these vows vanished like the dew before the rising sun, and left poor Helena trailing like a discarded pet.

But Helena would not give up, and she was desperate to find some favour, however small, in Demetrius' eyes. Learning from Hermia and Lysander of their plan to flee from Athens the following night, she resolved to tell Demetrius and lead him to where the lovers had arranged to meet, by moonlight, in the wood . . .

These final days of the slow-waning moon had others in a flurry besides our tangled lovers.

In a workman's house in Athens six men were gathered, six honest, earnest, hard-working men of that great city. There was Peter Quince the carpenter, Francis Flute the bellow's mender, Tom Snout the tinker, Robin Starveling the tailor, Snug the joiner; and last, but by no means least, Nick Bottom the weaver.

They planned a most important event for the celebrations of Duke Theseus' wedding day: a play, performed by them. And what a play their play would be! A story of tragic lovers such as there had never been in all the world: 'The most lamentable comedy and cruel death of Pyramus and Thisby': a very good piece of work, Bottom assured the assembled company, and helpfully urged Peter Quince to start by calling them, man by man, according to the parts that they would play.

Bottom the weaver was, in the eyes of all who knew him, a most worthy man, a man of many parts and many talents, a man who,

amongst all the quantities of working men in Athens, *must* play Pyramus, the lover that kills himself for love . . .

Bottom was pleased with this. Why, it would call for a truly *dramatic* performance. It would draw tears in torrents from the audience, though he confessed he was more disposed to play a tyrant, for a tyrant could rant and rave. He leapt to his feet and bellowed lustily,

'The raging rocks
And shivering shocks
Shall break the locks
Of prison gates . . .'

Now this was a part a man was made for! (A lover, he assured his friends, was more condoling . . .)

Francis Flute was none too pleased to have to play the lady's part, for he had a beard coming.

'Let me play Thisby too!' cried Bottom with considerable relish. 'I'll speak in a monstrous little voice. "Thisne, Thisne," ' he demonstrated his tiny squeak with much flapping of 'elegant' lady's wrists, ' "Pyramus my lover dear! Thy Thisby dear and lady dear!" '

The other parts were distributed with greater speed, for Bottom's imagination was not truly captured by mere fathers or mothers of the tragic lovers. But the *lion* – that was a part! If Snug the joiner was nervous of it, Bottom would do it! He would roar such a roar that the Duke would say 'Let him roar again!' Or, if that frightened the ladies in the audience, he could roar as gently as a dove, as sweetly as a nightingale . . .

It was, however, firmly established by good Peter Quince (who manfully wrestled control of the proceedings from the enthusiastic weaver), that Bottom must play *Pyramus*. This Pyramus was as sweet-faced a man as any you would see on a summer's day, a most gentleman-like man . . .

Bottom's thoughts had turned to the question of the beard. What beard should Pyramus wear, he mused. Your straw-coloured beard?

Your orange-tawny beard? Your purple-in-grain beard, your
French crown-coloured beard, your perfect yellow?

With some effort, Quince managed to move on, for he
had a final, most important communication to impart
to his attentive company They must *learn their lines*. By
tomorrow night, they must all know them well. (Snug
took this particularly seriously, for he was slow to
learn, and was concerned to get the lion's roaring
right.)

And so as not to have the whole of Athens know
their plans, they would rehearse their play in secret.
In the woods outside the town, they would all
meet the following night, by moonlight . . .

The wood lay silver-tipped beneath the moon,
each blade of grass, each leaf and branch
soft-stroked with liquid pearl. It was a place
of whisperings and shimmerings, of watching
eyes green-glowing like fire beneath the
giant trees.

It was a place of magic. It was bewitched
by more than the moon's caress across the
darkened glades.

It was the realm of Oberon, King of Fairies,
and of Titania, his silver queen. No human eye
could see them, no human ear could hear them,
but they were there, woven in the rugged oaks that
bowed across the moon-washed world, threaded in
the murmuring earth, floating on the lilt of brooks
and the sweet wind that sighed across the leaves.

And tonight this wood was haunted by more than
the joyous revels of fairies, elves and sprites, for it
trembled beneath the King of Fairies' anger at the
Fairy Queen.

Titania had, as her attendant, a lovely human boy
taken from an Indian king. How she loved and cherished
this changeling child! But Oberon was jealous: he desired the
boy to be a knight of his train, to wander the wild forests with *him* . . .

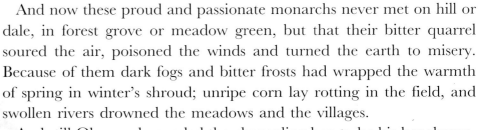

And now these proud and passionate monarchs never met on hill or dale, in forest grove or meadow green, but that their bitter quarrel soured the air, poisoned the winds and turned the earth to misery. Because of them dark fogs and bitter frosts had wrapped the warmth of spring in winter's shroud; unripe corn lay rotting in the field, and swollen rivers drowned the meadows and the villages.

And still Oberon demanded the changeling boy to be his henchman, and still Titania withheld him, crowned him with flowers and made him all her joy. Now, though they flew from the far corners of the earth to bring their blessings to Duke Theseus' wedding day, still their old quarrel flared anew . . .

'Ill met by moonlight, proud Titania!' Oberon hailed her, and the great oaks trembled with the anger of this powerful lord of the dark place, while all his tiny elves drew close behind their master.

Titania's fairies peeped from the silver glow that wrapped their dancing queen.

'What, jealous Oberon,' Titania cried. 'Fairies, skip away. I have foresworn his bed and company!'

He stepped towards her, fierce. 'Why should Titania cross her Oberon?' he challenged her again. 'I do but beg a little changeling boy to be my henchman!'

'The fairy land buys not the child from me!' Titania sang and danced away from the dark thunder of her husband's eyes. 'His mother was of my following; for her sake I do rear up her boy, and for her sake I will not part with him!' And away she flew, her lilting voice echoing in Oberon's ears with mocking taunt.

He brooded on her disobedience, and the brooding filled his soul. *She* would not leave this forest glade till he had tormented her for his injury! He called his attendant to him, a shrewd, prick-eared goblin known as Puck, much given to pranks and roguish tricks. To him, the King of Fairies gave his secret orders. There was a tiny purple flower called 'love-in-idleness' that grew far off in the western lands . . .

'Fetch me that flower,' he breathed. 'The juice of it laid on sleeping eyelids will make man or woman madly love the next live creature that it sees. I'll watch Titania when she is asleep, and drop the liquid on her eyes. The next thing that she, waking, looks upon, be it lion, bear, wolf or bull, meddling monkey or busy ape, she shall pursue it with the soul of love . . . Fetch me this herb, and be here again before the whale can swim a league!'

'I'll put a girdle round about the earth in forty minutes!' chanted Puck, and disappeared.

And Oberon brooded on his plan; while Titania languished in bewitchment, he could spirit away the changeling boy . . .

But Oberon's mischievous thoughts were suddenly and violently disturbed: a raucous clamour tore the air, the sound of quarrelling *human* voices, the crash of *human* feet! Being invisible, he hovered close to hear these rash intruders entering his domain.

It was Demetrius, blundering through the undergrowth in search of Hermia. But he was followed, as he always was, by love-lorn Helena. In vain he tried to shake her off. He yelled. He frowned. He shouted. But she was there, her love-sick gaze still drinking in each word and look of his as though they were the nectar of the gods themselves.

'I cannot love you!' he shouted, for perhaps the hundredth time.

'And even for that I do love you more,' she sobbed. 'I am your slave, the more you beat me, I will fawn on you. Use me but as your slave, spurn me, strike me, neglect me, only give me leave to follow you . . .'

'I am sick when I must look at you,' the desperate youth declared.

'And I am sick when I look not at you,' the wretched girl replied.

And Oberon, festering with his own lovers' quarrel, was touched by the unhappy Helena's plight. He vowed a second vow that night: before Helena could leave his forest realm, Demetrius would seek her love and she would fly from him.

Now Puck alighted at his side and held aloft the magic flower. Oberon seized it. It caught a glancing moonbeam and gleamed purple in the cloaking dark. He stroked it, murmuring, and the wind took up his words and sowed them in the trees . . . 'I know a bank where the wild thyme blows, where oxlips and the nodding violet grows. There sleeps Titania sometime of the night, lulled in these flowers . . .'

And then, with sudden anger he cried out, 'With the juice of this I'll streak her eyes and make her full of hateful fantasies!'

His gaze now fell on eager Puck, ever ready to follow his master's wish. 'Take some of it,' he ordered him. 'Seek through this grove. A sweet Athenian lady is in love with a disdainful youth. Anoint his eyes with this, and do it when the next thing that he spies will be the lady. You shall know the man by the Athenian clothes that he has on.'

Titania slept, while fairy sentinels drooped drowsily and did not see the Fairy King creep close to her, nor see him squeeze the magic juice across her eyes, nor hear his murmured words . . .

'What thou seest when thou dost wake,
Do it for thy true love take
Love and languish for his sake
Be it lynx, or cat, or bear
Leopard, or boar with bristled hair.
Wake when some vile thing is near.'

Below the sleeping Fairy Queen two other lovers came into the glade: Lysander and the beautiful Hermia, now much begrimed and stuck with twigs and leaves. They had lost their way in this strange wood, and now they were foot-sore and desperately craved sleep. In the morning, fresh, they could resume their flight from Athens.

'Good night, sweet friend,' Hermia whispered to Lysander. 'May your love never alter until your sweet life ends.'

'Amen to that fair prayer,' the loving youth replied. 'And let my life end when I end loyalty . . .'

They settled down together in that dappled glade (but not too close together, till the bonds of marriage were tied up). And so it came about that wandering Puck, seeking Demetrius and Helena, now came upon *this* sleeping couple. He noted the youth's Athenian clothes and the young woman lying some little way away: at once he assumed *this* was the young woman so churlishly rejected by the youth that Oberon had seen. Swiftly he poured the magic juice across Lysander's eyes, and sped back to his master's side.

For a moment the glade was quiet. And then the crashing in the undergrowth began again; into the glade stumbled frantic Demetrius, still running from a more than frantic Helena. With a final furious shout at her, he plunged on into the wood, so that she stood now, quite alone amid the looming trees.

It seemed now that no plea, no prayer could work its charm on scornful Demetrius, and Helena despaired. She ached with tiredness. She slipped and slithered in the dark, seeking a place where she could sink to rest. As she did, she stumbled across sleeping Lysander. Afraid he might be hurt, she shook the youth, and Lysander, waking with his eyes streaked with the magic juice,

saw Helena and fell instantly, passionately, in love. All thoughts
of Hermia took flight (how tedious seemed the hours spent with
her). Who could still love a raven such as Hermia beside this
glowing, dove-like Helena?

Helena stared at Lysander now in greater misery than ever
before. What had she done to draw this mockery from others? It
was not enough for Demetrius to spurn her, but Lysander must add
to her injuries by playing his own games with her! It was too much
for any girl to bear! And Helena rushed frantically from the glade,
Lysander in hot pursuit of this, his most passionate new love.

Hermia, quite ignorant of the magic changes in her lover's
heart, slept on, until a dream of crawling serpents woke her
violently. Alone? Lysander gone? No answering shout to
greet her? Only a thousand night creatures' glinting eyes!

In terror she ran off, shrieking for Lysander . . .

To this same wood, at midnight, came the six working men of
Athens, prepared to do their play exactly as they would before
Duke Theseus. They tramped into the moonlit glade and looked
around (a little apprehensively, if each were to admit it to the other).

'Here's a marvellous convenient place for our rehearsal,'
Quince declared. 'This green plot shall be our stage, this hawthorn
bush our dressing room.'

Bottom had been thinking very seriously. 'There are things in
this comedy of Pyramus and Thisby that will never please,' he
told them, soberly. 'First, Pyramus must draw a sword to kill
himself, which the ladies of the audience cannot abide . . .'

Snout, Starveling and Flute all nodded: the killing must,
undoubtedly, be quite left out.

Bottom had pondered his way towards a better answer. They
must have an introduction to their play – a *prologue* (he said the
word proudly to give it full effect) – and this prologue would say
that they would do no harm with their swords, and that Pyramus
was not really killed, and (to reassure them thoroughly) Pyramus
was not *really* Pyramus, but Bottom the weaver.

An excellent solution!

In the trees about their makeshift stage there lurked an unseen
watcher who observed their earnest efforts with amusement.

'What hempen homespuns have we swaggering here, so near the cradle of the Fairy Queen?' bright Puck enquired, for his mischievous nose had sniffed out the flavour of some teasing frolic for his entertainment.

Unknowing of their hidden audience, the players now began. Bottom, as Pyramus, was first. 'Thisby, the flowers of odious savours sweet,' he declared, most eloquently.

'*Odours, odours,*' interrupted Quince.

'Odours savours sweet,' said Bottom obligingly. 'But hark! A voice!' and right on cue, he disappeared into the hawthorn bush.

There was a silence. All eyes turned expectantly to Francis Flute. It dawned on him, though slowly, that they were all waiting for *him.*

'Must I speak now?' he asked, nervously.

'Aye,' said Quince, most patiently. 'Pyramus goes but to see a noise, and will come again.'

Promptly (before he lost his nerve), Flute spewed out all his lines at once in a great flood, and left nothing more to speak in the rest of the play.

Quince sighed deeply; 'You must not speak that yet,' he said, in a tone of utmost world-weariness, 'Pyramus, enter!' he called. 'Your cue is past . . .'

But hovering Puck had suddenly devised the merriest prank of all. Following Bottom into the hawthorn bush, he had swiftly touched the weaver's ears, which, in no more than the blinking of a goblin's eye became long, furry, flapping ears; his nose, which grew into a long, bony nose; his eyes, which became the large, dark, somewhat bewildered eyes of an enormous, hairy ass!

Bottom, unaware of this miraculous transformation, reappeared at Quince's call with gusto.

'If I were fair, Thisby,' he announced with passion, 'I were only yours!'

His companions stared. They blinked. They backed away. They trembled. And then, with one panic-stricken howl, they fled.

Somewhat bewildered, Bottom watched his friends run out, run back again, stare, shriek, point fingers, gibber, peer at him from behind the trees and disappear again . . .

Why did they run? Some joke of theirs, to come and gawp and run again!

'Bless you, bless you, Bottom, bless you!' Quince whispered in awe.
'You are transformed!'

This was unmistakeably a ruse to frighten him, Bottom decided.
If only they could! He looked about him at the giant trees,
standing sentinel about the grove. They loomed, they leaned . . .

He shook himself. 'I will not stir from this place,' he
declared. 'Do what they can, I will not stir. I will walk
up and down here. And I will sing. And they shall
hear I am not afraid!' this last he yelled defiantly
across the silent grove. And he burst forth,

>   'The ousel cock so black of hue
>   With orange-tawny bill
>   The throstle . . .'

Cushioned on her bed of flowers, Titania stirred, then
stretched and woke. And as she did, her eyes, charmed by
the flower-juice, fell on this valiant figure with the head of
a great ass and body of a sturdy, somewhat portly, man; and
instantly this queen of gossamer light fell wildly, insanely, in
love with him.

'What angel wakes me from my flowery bed?' she breathed.

The object of her adoration stamped on across the grove, thump,
thump, thump, thump; then back again, clump, clump, clump, clump,
and then he bellowed even louder to warn the looming shades of night
they could not threaten him.

>   'The finch, the sparrow and the lark
>   The plain-song cuckoo grey . . .' he carolled.

And then he stopped, for now he saw the silver vision decked in
moonbeams float across the grove, and heard her, with a voice like
tinsel bells of flowers, speak to him . . .

'I pray you, gentle mortal, sing again. Mine ear is much enchanted
by thy note. So is mine eye enthralled by thy shape . . . and I am
moved to say that I do love thee.'

Bottom was not a man ever at a loss for long. He prided himself on
this. Silver visions who sang of love in moonlit woods notwithstanding,
he *would* maintain his true sense of proportion at all times . . .

'I love you,' the lady sang.

'I think, mistress,' he said, sensibly, 'you should have little reason for
that; and yet, to say the truth, reason and love keep little company
together nowadays . . .'

'Thou art as wise as thou art beautiful,' the wondrous lady murmured.

'Not so, neither,' he assured her, 'but if I had wit enough to get out of this wood . . .'

'Thou shalt not go,' her music voice sang on. 'Thou shalt remain here, for I do *love* thee . . . Therefore go with me,' the lady whispered in his ear (the great, tall ass's ear that twitched a little for her lips were tickling him). And away she drew him, and wove her spells about him: she would give him fairies to attend on him and grant his every wish; he could sleep on heady flowers while their perfumes wafted him to sleep; he could feed on apricots and dewberries, on purple grapes and mulberries, on honeybags stolen from the bumble bees; her fairies would fan moonbeams from his sleeping eyes with wings of butterflies.

Bottom, refusing to be bewildered by the orderly procession of tiny fairies before his eyes, was always a polite man. Each one, in turn, he addressed with courteous concentration, made sure he asked each name, and shook each hand (though this was somewhat difficult with hands that seemed to slip like moonlight through his fingers).

'Tie up my love's tongue,' the silver lady whispered. 'Bring him silently . . .'

Oberon's eyes danced with delight at Titania's new love, for quickly Puck had flown to tell his master, and to amuse him, too, with tales of how he led the other workmen a merry caper from the woods, scrambling and slithering as they were through briars and thorns to escape that haunted place.

And here, to add to Oberon's delight, came the Athenians. Swiftly the dark king and his impish henchman vanished, to watch the spectacle unseen.

Young Hermia came flying in, pursued by passionate Demetrius. She, though much irritated by the persistence of this unwanted youth, was more concerned at the disappearance of her love, Lysander. A thought struck her: Demetrius had killed him! She rounded on this hapless youth, her dark eyes flashing instant vengeance if this was so.

Demetrius gave up. He was growing a little weary of this chase, for it gave so few rewards. He was exhausted by these endless hours chasing through this endless wood. Foot-weary, and in great ill-humour, he left Hermia to run on, and lay down on the ground, to sleep.

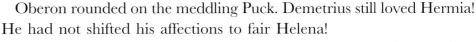

Oberon rounded on the meddling Puck. Demetrius still loved Hermia! He had not shifted his affections to fair Helena!

No, Puck admitted (much amused by this spectacle of squabbling humans), this was not the Athenian he had charmed . . .

'About the wood go swifter than the wind,' Oberon gave orders, angrily. 'Find Helena of Athens. Lead her here, by magic.' And while Puck flew off to do his bidding, Oberon alighted on the ground near Demetrius, and swift as wind he charmed Demetrius' eyes in time for Helena's appearance.

Puck was much enjoying himself, for mischief was the food of life to him. In a twinkling of an eye he was back, to sing,

> 'Captain of our fairy band,
> Helena is here at hand.
> And the youth, mistook by me . . .
> *Lord, what fools these mortals be!'*

Two youths, who both loved Hermia, to be translated into two who both loved Helena! No greater fun could Puck imagine!

Helena's bewilderment at Lysander's loud vows of undying love had turned to fierce indignation. She was desperate to get away from him, to escape this cruel mockery. Stumbling in the moonlight across the forest glade, Lysander close behind, she fell across Demetrius. He woke, and saw the woman he had scorned so bitterly now coloured by the love-flower's enchanted mists.

'Helen, goddess, nymph, perfect, divine!' he cried. 'To what, my love, shall I compare your eyes? Crystal is muddy! Oh, let me kiss this princess of pure white, this seal of bliss!'

Helena fell back in disbelief. They were hell bent to use her for their merriment! It was not enough that Demetrius should hate her, as he had made plain, now he joined with Lysander to taunt her pitilessly!

'You would not use a gentle lady so,' she begged, 'to vow and swear your love when I am sure you hate me in your hearts. You are both rivals and love Hermia. Now both rivals you mock Helena!'

To simplify this tangled knot, Lysander grandly donated the absent Hermia (whom he no longer loved) to Demetrius.

Demetrius, who had loved Hermia wildly until a few moments ago, now scorned the gift. He loved *Helena*, adored *Helena*, would worship *Helena* for ever more.

Into this hornets' nest came Hermia, still fretting at Lysander's disappearance from her side, yet with his vows of loyalty to her still echoing in her ears. She saw him now and rushed to his side. 'Why did you leave me so unkindly?'

But why should he stay, she heard Lysander's cold and unfamiliar voice. Love drew him on!

She stopped. She looked from him to Helena, from Helena to Demetrius. She heard again these words her ears could not believe. Her own true love's lips now shouting at her to go and leave him, declaring the *hate* he felt for her!

Helena, watching this extraordinary scene, saw it all clearly now. It was a plot between all three of them! *Hermia* was at the root of it. This *friend*, with whom she had shared all vows of childhood, was locked in conspiracy with these cruel men, to scorn and bait her!

'Oh, is it all forgotten? All school-days' friendship, childhood innocence?' she sobbed.

Hermia stopped the stream of words. 'I do not scorn you, it seems you scorn me!' In disbelief she heard Lysander's voice. 'My love, my life, my soul, fair Helena! Helen I love you, by my life I do.'

And then Demetrius, bristling against his rival, 'I say I love you more than he can do!'

'If you say so,' Lysander shouted, 'withdraw and prove it!'

'Quick, come!' Demetrius yelled, and drew his sword.

Now Hermia understood. She rounded on her friend. 'You juggler! You canker-blossom! You thief of love! What, have you come by night and stolen my love's heart from him?'

'You counterfeit! You puppet!' shrieked Helena back, convinced that this was all still part of their dreadful plot.

'Puppet!' bellowed Hermia. 'Now I see she compares our heights! With her personage, her *tall* personage, her height, no less, she has won him!' She danced in rage before her willowy friend. 'And are you grown so high in his esteem because *I* am so dwarfish and so short? How short am I, you painted maypole? Speak! How short am I? I am not so short that my nails can't reach your eyes!'

'Let her not hurt me,' shrieked Helena. 'Let her not strike me. When she is angry she is keen and shrewd. She was a vixen when she went to school, and though she is little, she is fierce!'

'Little again! Nothing but little!' screamed Hermia, and flew at Helena. Lysander thrust shrinking Helena protectively behind him.

Demetrius shouted belligerently, 'Do not take Helena's part!' and once again they were circling each other, like spitting cats . . .

And then (so as not to use swords before the ladies) they went off to find a place to fight for Helena's love, still glaring wildly at each other.

Oberon looked at Puck, and his look was like the thunder before it erupts from a glowering sky.

'This is thy negligence!'

'Believe me, King of Shadows,' Puck sang out, 'I mistook . . . Did you not tell me I should know the man by the Athenian garments he had on? I have anointed an Athenian's eyes!' (But, mistake or not, what sport to see these mortals jangling!)

'These mortals seek a place to fight,' bellowed Oberon. 'Hurry and overcast the night with fog, black, black fog to lead these rivals far astray that they may never meet each other! Then crush this herb into Lysander's eye,' and his look allowed no meddling pranks or disobedience this time.

This miserable confusion must be set to rights and Lysander's vision turned from Helena to Hermia again. But haste, haste, for the night was paling fast, and all must be accomplished before the break of dawn . . .

The impish Puck did as his master ordered, gleefully. He danced and floated in the mists, calling now in Demetrius' voice to wandering Lysander, now in Lysander's voice to stumbling Demetrius; now in a bush, a tree, across the brook, now far behind, now far in front, now up, now down, egging each on until their legs grew weary, their flesh stung with pricks and scratches and each separately, ignorant of how close the other stumbled in the mists, lay down to sleep until daybreak could release them from this misery.

And then the ladies came: first, Helena, smeared with mud, her dress in shreds and longing now for nothing but the sunlight's warmth so that she could escape this hideous place and friends who detested her enough to play these cruel jokes. She lay down to sleep.

'Yet but three?' grinned hovering Puck.

'Come one more;

Two of both kinds

Makes up four.

Here she comes, cursed and sad!'

Hermia could go no further. Though she still longed to find Lysander and stop the fight, she was so soaked with dew, so torn with briars that she was almost crawling . . .

And she too lay down to sleep.

Now they were ready for Puck's magic: each close together, though they did not know it, each near their chosen love.

He dropped the herb on to Lysander's sleeping eyes.

'On the ground
Sleep sound
I'll apply
To your eye,
Gentle lover, remedy.

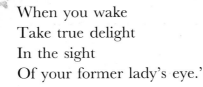

When you wake
Take true delight
In the sight
Of your former lady's eye.'

Invisible to the lovers' eyes, a stranger company than they could ever imagine now came among them.

'Come sit upon this flowery bed while I caress your cheeks and stick musk-roses in your sleek, smooth head, and kiss your fair, large ears, my gentle joy,' Titania's cooing voice enticed the weaver on.

Bottom was much enjoying this unlooked for holiday from the workaday existence of a sober Athens weaver.

'Where's Peaseblossom?' he asked. 'Scratch my head, good Peaseblossom. Where's Monsieur Cobweb? Good monsieur, fetch me a red-hipped bumble bee on the top of a thistle; and good monsieur, bring me the honeybag; and have a care that the honeybag does not break. I would be loath to have you overflown with a honeybag, signor.' He settled luxuriously into the bower of flowers. 'Where's Monsieur Mustardseed?'

'What's your will?' a tiny voice came to his languid ears.

'Nothing, good monsieur,' said Bottom generously, 'but to help Monsieur Peaseblossom scratch. I must go to the barber's, monsieur,' he assured him, seriously, 'for I think I am marvellously hairy about the face . . .'

He yawned. And if the wondrous fairy lady would cease her stroking and allow him, he was now ready to sleep . . .

'Sleep,' her voice was in the wind, and in the leaves, 'and I will wind thee in my arms. So does the woodbine entwine the sweet honeysuckle . . . Oh, how I love thee! How I do dote on thee!'

And Titania, too, slept, wound round her love. She did not know this passion was the work of jealous Oberon, nor that he had already seized the changeling boy while she lay wrapped in adoration of Bottom the weaver's ass-headed charms.

Their purpose won, two moon-dappled shadows came among the lovers to undo the charms. Oberon bent low across his queen and spoke the charmed words that would undo the spell that bound her. He called her, gently, 'Now, my Titania, wake, my sweet queen.'

She woke, and saw him bending over her, and looked about her, startled. 'My Oberon! What visions I have seen! I thought I loved an ass.'

'There lies thy love,' murmured Oberon, and as she backed in horror from poor Bottom, blissfully ass-headed on the ground, the King of Fairies took her hand.

'Come my queen, take hands with me, and rock the ground whereon these sleepers be!' And so these monarchs of the moonlit night joined hands, new-tied in bonds of love, and dancing in a magic circle blessed the sleepy lovers on the ground.

Tomorrow night their fairy dance would bless the triumph of Duke Theseus' wedding day, but as the morning lark raised his shrill cry, they vanished, to follow the shades of night to other lands . . .

With the morning lark came others to that forest glade. Duke Theseus and his bride-to-be Hippolyta were revelling in their long-awaited wedding day. Before daybreak they had risen to follow the hounds and hunting horns into the woods, and they stood now, listening to their swelling music across the hills and valleys. They paused in the sunlit glade to catch the scent of morning in the flowers, and stumbled, much to their surprise, on the four lovers, fast asleep and lying close together on the ground.

'Go bid the huntsman wake them with their horns,' Duke Theseus commanded.

To the triumphant bay of unleashed hounds and bray of horns across the western valley, the startled lovers woke. They stared at the wondering audience, looked at each other, tried to stammer out an explanation of their presence there, but found they could not really find one . . .

'I came with Hermia,' Lysander remembered, suddenly, and turned with love towards her. All memories of adoration felt for Helena had flown with waking sight of Hermia . . .

And by some power which he could not understand, Demetrius now found himself in love with Helena and not with Hermia!

And so they stood there, once four lovers running in a ring about a moonlit wood, now two loving pairs: Lysander and Hermia, Demetrius and Helena, who still could not believe her ears were not playing tricks on her when she heard Demetrius' declaration of his love for her before the *Duke*! 'All the faith, the virtue of my heart, the object and the pleasure of my eye is only Helena,' he said!

Duke Theseus saw at once how perfectly the tangled knot had been untied, and how the thorny problems set by Hermia's father were now resolved. It was a splendid outcome for his own, most glorious, wedding day, and he was in no mood to let a father's anger at the thwarting of his wishes mar its pleasures or the happiness of these young people, so in love.

Swiftly he decided. He would overrule the father if he was still disposed to press an unwanted marriage on his reluctant daughter. 'In the temple, by and by with us, these couples shall eternally be knit in marriage,' he said. 'Away with us to Athens! Three and three we'll hold a feast in great solemnity!'

And with his bride-to-be upon his arm, he swept from the sunlit glade, leaving the bewildered lovers quite alone. They looked at each other curiously. Each wondered if the others had heard and seen what they *thought* they had seen in this strange and misty night just passed . . .

'These things seem small and indistinguishable, like far-off mountains turned into clouds,' murmured Demetrius, wonderingly.

'I seem to see these things with parted eye, when everything seems double,' said Hermia.

'And I have found Demetrius, like a jewel, my own,' sang Helena, who could think of nothing else.

'Are you sure that we are awake?' Demetrius still wondered. 'It seems to me that yet we sleep, we dream.'

And yet Duke Theseus *had* been there, *had* bid them follow him to Athens. On that they all agreed.

They linked arms, chattering suddenly like magpies about the night's events, and followed the Duke's party from that forest glade.

The glade was silent now, warm-lit by morning sun. Gone were the flitting shadows of the night who flew on moonbeams from tree to tree. Gone were the lovers, babbling of their dream.

The sun blazed down and wrapped the sleeping Bottom in its golden blanket. He dreamed on, and on. He mumbled in his sleep. He murmured softly, laughed, stretched, and laughed again.

And then slowly, he began to wake, luxuriously. 'When my cue comes, call me, and I will answer,' he murmured. 'My next is, "Most fair Pyramus . . ." ' He stretched again. Then he sat up. He looked about him. No one there? He called, 'Peter Quince! Flute! Snout! God's my life, stolen away and left me asleep!'

Then he remembered: a woman of silver light who stroked him, loved him, sang to him, and he wafting on sweet beds of flowers, her king! A life of song and drowsy luxury, of idleness beyond his dreams . . . He almost swooned again with memories.

'I have had a most rare vision,' he assured himself. 'I have had a dream, past the wit of man to say what dream it was. I thought I was . . .' he shook the thought away. 'There is no man can tell what,' he announced conclusively to the slumbering wood. 'I thought I had . . .' he began again.

And again he shook his head. 'The eye of man has not heard, the ear of man has not seen, man's hand is not able to taste, his tongue to imagine or his heart to report, what my dream was,' he addressed the

brooding oaks . . . and for a
moment he was wandering in his
dream again, lost in its ecstasies . . .
'I will get Peter Quince to write a ballad
of this dream,' he announced with more
certainty, 'and it shall be called Bottom's
dream, because it has no bottom . . .'

At Quince's house Bottom's friends despaired.
A play without Nick Bottom? A play without their
Pyramus? Bottom was the Pyramus to beat all Pyramuses,
the tragic lover to beat all lovers. They trembled to think what might have
happened to him. Had he been carried off by spirits, transformed
(before their eyes) into a monster? Or was it all a nightmare they
would wake from, happily?

'Where are these lads?' the booming tones of Bottom sang along the
street. 'Where are these good fellows?'

They gaped, searched wildly for the ass's head they had last seen on
him. Seeing nothing but their good friend's jovial face, they promptly
leapt with joy, clapped him on the back, danced several jigs around
him, and all at once there was a flurry of excited preparations.

Costumes ready? Strings to their beards? 'Let Thisby have clean
clothes,' urged Bottom enthusiastically. 'And let him that plays the lion
not cut his nails, for they shall hang out like the lion's claws. And, most
dear actors,' he called them back, 'eat no onions nor garlic, for we are
to utter sweet breath; and I do not doubt but to hear them say, it is a
sweet comedy. No more words! Away! Go! Away!'

The lovers came now, wed, to while away the hours before their
wedding night with jovial entertainment: and a jovial entertainment it
certainly promised to be: 'A tedious brief scene of young Pyramus and
his love Thisby; very tragical mirth,' the company of actors announced
themselves.

The young couples settled comfortably, prepared to be much amused
by the efforts of these earnest working men who had so worked to
bring this 'tragic' tale to Theseus' celebration.

They little knew what scenes of mirthful tragedy *they* had played

before another audience in a silver wood not so very far away . . .

Wall came first. With trembling wide-eyed face above the chink made by his parted fingers, he explained this was the hole through which the tragic lovers Pyramus and Thisby would whisper secretly.

'Would you desire a wall to speak better?' Duke Theseus enquired of his fellow watchers approvingly.

They hushed as Pyramus crept in, soft-footed, and with much staring gloomily about him to ensure there was no doubt he came in *dangerous* secrecy.

'Oh grim-looked night! Oh night with hue so black!

Oh night which ever is when day is not!' he wailed.

'Oh wall oh sweet lovely wall!

Show me thy chink to blink through with mine eyes!'

Dutifully Wall held up two fingers.

'Thanks, courteous Wall,' said Bottom with tears of heartfelt gratitude in his eyes. He peered through the chink.

'But what see I? No Thisby do I see!' he rolled his eyes and clutched his heart.

'Oh wicked Wall!' he beat the Wall's sturdy breast (Wall staggered a little beneath the impassioned onslaught but withstood it sturdily). 'Cursed be thy stones for thus deceiving me.'

'I think the Wall being able to talk, should curse again,' Theseus whispered rather loudly to Hippolyta.

'No! In truth sir he should not!' Bottom was most perturbed to find there was some confusion on this point. ' "Deceiving me" is Thisby's cue,' he explained patiently to the confused Duke. 'She is to enter now and I am to spy her through the wall. You shall see . . . here she comes!'

Unfortunately for Bottom, Francis Flute was having a little trouble with his yellow wig. It would fly off whenever he tried to move. He clasped it firmly to his head and lolloped on, kicking the folds of his dress valiantly aside (though he had quite forgotten to change his boots).

Suddenly, and alarmingly, he was facing this distinguished audience. He peered owlishly at them, trembled with the seriousness of his forth-coming task, and squeaked determinedly.

'Oh Wall, my cherry lips have often kissed thy stones.'

'I see a voice,' gasped Pyramus, relieved to see his partner finally appear beyond the looming shape of Wall. 'Now will I to the chink!'

At this most poetic exclamation, the audience, who had been merely tittering, now dissolved in uncontrollable laughter.

'Oh kiss me through the hole of this vile wall,' shrieked Pyramus, now much enjoying himself and gathering momentum since the audience seemed to be having so much fun . . .

'I kiss the wall's hole, not your lips at all,' piped Thisby.

'Wilt thou at Ninny's tomb meet me straight away?' yelled Pyramus.

'I come without delay,' lisped Thisby from beneath the crooked wig, for it had now slid disconcertingly across one eye.

And out they marched, arm in arm, forgetting they were still two lovers separated by a wall . . .

Wall, left alone before a giggling audience, shuffled from foot to foot, summoned what remaining courage he had and belted out his lines at top speed.

'Thus have I, Wall, my part discharged, and being done, thus Wall away doth go!' and without further ado, he fled.

The audience waited expectantly. Lion came on (Snug's face peering reassuringly from beneath the shaggy head), and spoke a pretty speech to explain he was really Snug the joiner, and no fierce lion.

'A very gentle beast,' Duke Theseus approved, 'and of a good conscience.'

Now it was Moonshine's turn. Much encouraged by the loud noises emitting from the audience, he waved his lantern enthusiastically and yelled, 'This lantern presents the horned moon. Myself the man in the moon do seem to be!'

On cue, Thisby clumped in, saw the lion, who duly roared a mighty roar. Thisby ran off shrieking, then ran on again, propelled by Peter Quince, to throw her cloak down on the ground. Lion seized the cloak, and with several lusty roars, tore it to shreds. Pyramus rushed on, saw the mangled cloak, assumed his lover Thisby dead, whipped out his sword, plunged it in his own breast, and fell moaning and grimacing with pain.

> 'Now am I dead
> Now am I fled
> My soul is in the sky
> Tongue, lose thy light
> Moon take thy flight!'

Though this last was not in the script as he remembered it, Moonshine took Pyramus at his word, and galloped off.

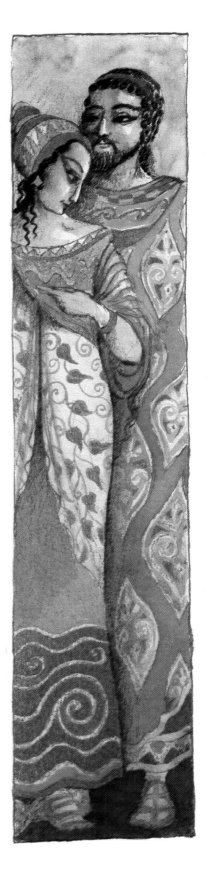

Thisby, wig restored, rushed on.

> 'What, dead my dove?
> Oh Pyramus, arise, speak, speak.
> Quite dumb?
> These lily lips, this cherry nose,
> These yellow cowslip cheeks,' she intoned, warming

greatly to the scene now that the play was nearly done.

And so the tragedy of Pyramus and Thisby galloped to its close, affording its audience no less transports of mirth and sheer delight than the antics of that same audience had once offered the sprightly Puck in that far-off, dream-washed, moonlit world outside the walls of Athens.

The palace was now quiet. The newly-weds had all retired to bed, wrapped in the magic of their love. And now a different magic came to touch Duke Theseus and his bride Hippolyta.

It was at first only a shimmering, and then a gentle whispering, a silver breeze that stirred across the halls, the kissing touch of shadows dancing with tinsel sounds across the moonbeams in the rooms . . .

They came, the King of Fairies and his queen, with all their train of fairies, elves and sprites led by bright Puck, to bring their blessing to this house and all who slept in it . . .

Or was it no more than a moonlit dream from an enchanted midsummer night?

Julius Caesar

Julius Caesar
ruler of the Roman Empire

Calpurnia
his wife

A soothsayer -
who foresees the future

Brutus

Cassius

Mark Antony

Octavius Caesar

Rome awaited the mighty Caesar, its streets and squares seething with citizens eager to hail a leader's triumph. And Caesar was no ordinary leader. He had defeated the rival general, Pompey. He had fought off the threat to his supremacy from Pompey's sons. Now Julius Caesar held undisputed sway in Rome: dictator for life, commander of the Roman army, the most powerful man in all the ancient world. He ruled unchallenged.

But there were those in Rome who did not celebrate. They mourned great Pompey's loss and loathed to see the people who had rejoiced at Pompey passing through the city, applauding now at Caesar's triumph over Pompey's blood. Decked out in holiday clothes, Rome's people poured into the streets to strew the ground with flowers and decorate the statues in Julius Caesar's honour.

It seemed the citizens of Rome were ripe to applaud any leader's triumph . . .

Into the streets strode Caesar, flanked by smiling senators and borne along amidst a jubilant mob of people, to shouts and cries of merriment and trumpets heralding the running race through Rome in celebration of this feast day.

The runners poised to begin. Caesar gave the signal. There was a joyful flourish from the trumpets.

'Caesar!' a voice shrilled above the trumpet's song. 'Caesar!'

Caesar paused. 'Who calls? I hear a tongue cry "Caesar!" Speak, Caesar is turned to hear.'

Again the wailing cry, shriller than any trumpet's note, 'Beware the Ides of March . . .'

'What man is that?' demanded Caesar. 'Set him before me; let me see his face.'

A flurry of movement amongst the crowd: a man fell forwards, stumbling before the dictator. He was old, and bent, and lined. He raised his eyes to Caesar's, and in them was the haunted look of one who gazes painfully into the future and reads the fates of men.

'Speak once again!' commanded Caesar.

'Beware the Ides of March!' the old man's cry pierced the restless hubbub of the crowd . . . and suddenly there was a hush. The Ides of March: the fifteenth day of March. Today was already the first day of that month! Now all were watching.

The silence grew, a creeping chill across the day's bright warmth.

All waited. Caesar stared into the crumpled parchment of the old man's face.

And then he turned his back, 'He is a dreamer; let us leave him: pass.' Within a moment Caesar had swept on, leaving the old man swallowed in the crowd that surged after the dictator along the narrow streets, even more buoyant on the wings of merriment than before and eager for the celebration games.

There was one senator who lingered behind the departing crowd with other thoughts to occupy his mind. With saddened eyes he watched the progress of this mighty leader along the clamorous street. Brutus mourned Caesar's rise to power as he might mourn a death: but it was not in sadness at Pompey's loss.

Brutus loathed the rise to power of any single man: it was, he believed, the death of liberty. He dreamed of a glorious state of Rome ruled not by the whims and choices of a single, all-powerful man, but by the balanced wisdom of a collective senate. As he watched Julius Caesar stride from triumph to triumph as though nothing was strong enough to block his way, there was a twisting unease that clouded all of Brutus' waking hours; with the unease had come other thoughts that sat painfully within his mind, thoughts he almost dared not recognize . . .

As he wrestled with his thoughts, he too was watched, as carefully as he himself watched Caesar. His friend Cassius had seen Brutus' brooding mood and knew what troubled him.

A sudden shout and the triumphant peal of trumpets reached them. Brutus started, stung from his reverie. 'What does this shouting mean? I do fear the people choose Caesar for their king.'

'Aye, do you fear it?' murmured Cassius, moving closer. He paused, then said with care, 'Then must I think you would not have it so.'

'I would not, Cassius,' Brutus answered quietly, and sighed. 'Yet I love him well.' He looked along the street towards the clamour, as though he was again debating inwardly some painful course. And then he shook the thoughts away and turned to Cassius. He looked at him curiously, as though aware for the first time of the deliberate pattern of his friend's probing words.

'What is it that you would impart to me? If it be anything towards the general good, set honour in one eye and death in the other, and I will look on both indifferently: for I love the name of honour more than I fear death.'

'Well, honour is the subject of my story,' said Cassius. 'I cannot tell what you and other men think of this life, but for myself, I would as soon not be, as live to be in awe of such a thing as I myself.' He moved in front of Brutus to bar his onward movement along the street and force his close attention. 'I was born as free as Caesar; so were you: we both have fed as well, and we can both endure the winter's cold as well as he!' His eyes glittered and his voice grew sharp with scorn. 'And this man has now become a god, and Cassius is a wretched creature and must bend his body if Caesar carelessly nods to him . . .'

'Another general shout,' gasped Brutus, turning towards the distant uproar. 'I do believe that this applause is for some new honours that are heaped on Caesar!'

'Why, man,' Cassius burst out, 'he bestrides the narrow world like a Colossus, and we petty men walk under his huge legs and peep about to find ourselves dishonourable graves. The fault, dear Brutus, is in ourselves, that we are underlings. "Brutus" and "Caesar": what should be in that *Caesar*? Why should that name be sounded more than yours? Write them together, yours is as fair . . . weigh them, it is as heavy; conjure with them, Brutus will start a spirit as soon as Caesar!'

Again he compelled his friend's attention, refusing to let him turn away. 'When was there a time, when Rome was not famed with more than with *one man*? When could they say, till now, that her wide walls encompassed but *one man*?'

Brutus gazed into Cassius' face, and then away again. He passed a hand across his eyes, wearily. 'I have some notion of what you would work me to,' he murmured. And then he seemed to gather strength, and spoke with emphasis. 'What you have said, I will consider. What you have to say I will with patience hear, and find a time to hear and answer such high things.'

He paused. Caesar was returning, drawing the joyful multitudes with him. The celebration games were over.

But on the dictator's face there was the hot burn of anger . . . and his wife Calpurnia looked pale. It seemed that Mark Antony had run into the great market place to end the race, and there had offered a king's crown to Caesar!

Caesar had pushed the crown away. A second time Mark Antony had offered it, and then a third. Three times had Caesar rejected it, firmly, and each time the crowd had cheered . . .

But Caesar had been angered by the people's glee that he refused the crown, for in his heart he wanted to be king. The heat and crush and noise of people pressing close had suddenly sickened him, and his old illness rose . . . There, before them all, in the great market-place, during the celebrations of his triumph, he had plunged into an epileptic fit and fallen, foaming-mouthed, on to the ground.

Returning now along the street, he had recovered. But he saw Cassius was watching him. For a moment he returned the steady stare, and then he spoke quickly, privately, to Mark Antony by his side. 'That Cassius has a lean and hungry look; he thinks too much, such men are dangerous.'

'Fear him not, Caesar,' Mark Antony was confident. 'He's not dangerous. He is a noble Roman, and well disposed.'

Caesar shook his head. 'Such men as he be never at heart's ease while they behold a greater than themselves, and therefore they are very dangerous.' But now he shook the lingering gloom away, 'I rather tell you what is to be feared, than what I fear,' he asserted, 'for always I am Caesar!'

The night was wild, the sky blue-shot with lightning flame and thunder hammered like a war in heaven. The people talked of weird, unearthly happenings: a slave whose hand burned like twenty torches while his skin remained untouched, lions lurking around the Capitol . . .

Under cover of this monstrous night, Cassius gathered men to work a bloody and most terrible task: other senators who feared, loathed, or resented Caesar, and wished his power removed.

And under cover of this fuming night there were papers, forged by Cassius, thrown in at Brutus' window. All claimed to have been written by respected citizens. All spoke of the great faith Rome's people had in Brutus and their fear that Caesar aimed to be crowned as king. There were other letters pasted on the statue of Brutus' famous ancestor, Lucius Brutus, a hero who had rid Rome of its last king, the tyrant Tarquin. So, skilfully, did Cassius take Brutus' sense of honour, his love of Rome and hatred of all tyranny, and fashion them into a net to bind him into their conspiracy.

Brutus twisted in the snare. Since Cassius had first whet him against Caesar, he had not slept. Since that moment on the feastday of the first of March to this, the Ides of March, for all those fifteen long days, his inner struggle had not ceased. Was there any other way to stop the

dictator's ruthless climb to absolute power? His mind could show him none. Caesar wanted to be crowned. Once beneath that crown, how might he change, how might he use his power *against* the liberty of Rome and all her people? How might that man, feeling his unchallenged strength, lose all pity for his fellow men and become a tyrant?

Brutus knew no reason to suspect Caesar *would* abuse his power: and he had no personal cause to hate this man. On the contrary he loved and most respected him. But what might he *become*, climbing the ladder upwards? That was the question. And what must be done to prevent the rot?

'It must be by his death.' The words, once out, were no more comfortable than when they lurked unsaid below the surface of his mind. 'Think of him as a serpent's egg which, hatched, would, as his kind, grow mischievous, and let's kill him in his shell.' Still he wrestled with the thought. 'Between the acting of a dreadful thing and the first movement, all the interim is like a hideous dream . . .'

'Sir, Cassius is at the door, and he desires to see you,' his servant broke through Brutus' thoughts with difficulty.

'Is he alone?'

'No, sir, there are more with him. Their hats are plucked about their ears and half their faces buried in their cloaks.'

So they had come to him: in the dead of night, the conspiracy, the faction against Caesar, cloaked in fear against discovery . . .

They entered, Cassius, and six others. Only Cassius showed openly who he was. The others huddled, hidden.

'Do I know these men that come along with you?' demanded Brutus.

'Yes, every man of them,' Cassius assured him, 'and all men here honour you and wish that you had that opinion of your honour which every noble Roman has of you.' And swiftly Cassius drew Brutus off, to lay their plan before him and bind the final threads to hold him: a call once again on his nobility and honour, to urge him out of the mire of self-debate and into the urgency of action.

Brutus made up his mind. 'Give me your hands all over, one by one,' he said suddenly. No oaths to bind them to their task, he urged, only their honesty and honour to keep them firm . . . and so he shook their hands. Trebonius, Decius, Casca, Cinna, Cimber, every one a fellow senator.

Cassius interrupted. 'I think it is not sensible that Mark Antony, so well beloved of Caesar, should outlive Caesar: we shall find him a shrewd contriver. Let Antony and Caesar fall together.'

Brutus stopped him short. 'Our course will seem too bloody, Cassius, to cut the head off and then hack the limbs, like wrath in death and envy afterwards. Antony is but a limb of Caesar: let us be sacrificers, not butchers.' He stared beyond the hideous deed they planned towards the glorious future that would follow. 'We all stand up against the spirit of Caesar, and in the spirit of men there is no blood.' If only they could reach Caesar's spirit and not dismember Caesar! But alas, Caesar must bleed for it!

He turned with fierce conviction towards the other men. 'Gentle friends, let's kill him boldly, but not wrathfully; let's carve him as a dish fit for the gods, not hew him as a carcass fit for hounds . . . and for Mark Antony, think not of him. He can do no more than Caesar's arm when Caesar's head is off.'

'Yet I fear him,' insisted Cassius, 'for the great love he bears to Caesar . . .'

Brutus would hear no more of killing Antony. Morning light already warmed the sky, and soon this day to end the growing tyranny of Caesar would begin. It must be marred by no more than what they *had* to do.

Cassius obeyed. 'Friends, disperse yourselves: but all remember what you said and show yourselves true Romans!'

Brutus watched them go. Now the choice was made. Now, on this Ides of March, the inner war could stop. He had decided, and he had decided for the good of Rome and all its people.

Caesar had not slept that night: neither the ominous boom of thunder nor Calpurnia, his wife, had let him rest. Three times she had cried out in her sleep, 'Help! They murder Caesar!' for she had dreamed she saw his statue running blood, and many lusty Romans bathed their hands in it, smiling . . . She begged him not to leave the safety of his house today to go to the senate.

'The things that threatened me never looked but on my back; when they shall see the face of Caesar, they are vanished!' Caesar dismissed her fears. Nor would he let her talk of grisly sights seen by the night watchmen, or of the hideous shrieks like groans of dying men in battle which had filled the darkness of the turbulent night.

'Danger knows full well that Caesar is more dangerous than he: we

are two lions born in one day, and I the elder and more terrible. Caesar *shall* go forth today,' Caesar told Calpurnia.

'Do not,' Calpurnia begged on her knees. 'Call it my fear that keeps you in the house, and not your own. We'll send Mark Antony to the senate-house; and he shall say you are not well today.'

Caesar helped his wife up. As certainly as he had said a moment ago that he *would* go, he now said, 'For you, I will stay at home.'

But the conspirators had come to fetch him. They smiled at Caesar. They smiled at Calpurnia's fears, and told Caesar that her dream was not of horror, but a vision of good fortune: the statue spouting blood in which so many smiling Romans bathed showed that from great Caesar Rome would suck reviving blood, and that great men would press for tokens of the mighty leader!

They said that on this very day the senate had decided to bestow a crown on him! If he sent word he would not come, they might then change their minds! They might think, if he hid himself, that Caesar was afraid!

Caesar changed his mind. 'How foolish do your fears seem now, Calpurnia! I am ashamed I did yield to them. Give me my robe, for I will go. Good friends,' he urged the men who planned his death, 'go in and taste some wine with me; and we, like friends, will straightway go together.'

Caesar had reached the entrance to the senate-house. Around the steps clustered eager senators and on all sides men pressed forward with petitions and requests, with urgent cries for the dictator's attention to their pleas.

Among them stood the old man who had warned against the Ides of March.

Caesar saw him, and stopped. 'The Ides of March have come,' he told him, with a smile.

'Aye, Caesar; but not gone,' the voice shrilled above the tumult, and then was lost.

'Hail Caesar! Read this paper,' instantly another voice was raised, but in a moment it was pushed aside by other suitors for the dictator's ear. Urgently the first man persisted, 'Caesar, read mine first: for mine is a suit that touches Caesar nearer; read it instantly!'

'What touches me shall be last served,' said Caesar, generous in his self-denial. 'What, is the fellow mad?' he asked, as again the man pushed forward yelling, 'Delay not, read it instantly.' And with an irritated gesture of denial, he began to climb the stairs.

Thus did Julius Caesar push aside the last remaining hand of help, for on the paper in that hand were held the names of the conspirators and details of their plot against his life.

Now all pressed more noisily after him, waving petitions and yelling above their neighbours' pleas.

Behind the thronging crowd, Cassius and Brutus mounted the stairs. At Cassius' elbow another senator appeared. He leaned towards them, low-voiced and secretive, 'I wish your enterprise today might thrive,' and then he advanced smiling, towards Caesar. In consternation fast becoming panic, they stared after him. Their plot already known and *Caesar* about to hear of it!

'Brutus, what shall be done?' hissed Cassius. 'If this be known, Cassius or Caesar never shall turn back, for I will slay myself.'

'Cassius, be constant,' Brutus calmed him. 'They speak not of our purpose, for look, he smiles, and Caesar does not change.'

The moment of blank terror gone, Cassius breathed deep. Now nothing stood between them and their deadly task. Caesar was hemmed in by senators all talking urgently. Already their fellow conspirator Trebonius was drawing Mark Antony aside . . .

Last instructions whispered: 'Casca, you are the first that rears your hand,' Cassius reminded him. Metullus Cimber pushed his way to Caesar and presented his petition: a pardon for his banished brother Publius Cimber. Loudly Caesar rejected it. Brutus pressed closer and repeated the request. Still Caesar was adamant: no pardon. Cassius fell to his knees to add his voice.

Caesar, finding his decision still questioned, now grew angry. 'I could be well moved, if I were like you,' his tones boomed out above them. 'But I am constant as the northern star. The skies are painted with unnumbered sparks; they are all fire and every one does shine, but there's but one in all that holds his place: so it is in the world; men are flesh and blood, and apprehensive: yet I do know but one that unassailable holds on his rank, unshaked of motion: and that I am he. I was constant Cimber should be banished, and constant do remain to keep him so!'

'Oh Caesar . . .' came Cinna's cry.

'Begone!' said Caesar, still unmoved.

'Great Caesar . . .' pleaded Decius.

'Does not even Brutus kneel to no avail?' said Caesar angrily.

'Speak, hands, for me!' came Casca's rallying cry. And then the blow.

Caesar staggered beneath the dagger's stab and lifted up his hands to feel, in disbelief. Then a second, third, fourth, fifth . . . each chopped his sword or dagger down again, again, again.

And then the last.

Caesar raised his eyes in pain and shock to Brutus' face. Brutus stabbed.

'And you, Brutus,' Caesar moaned, and fell to the ground, writhed, and lay still.

It was done. Gored and bleeding at the base of Pompey's statue lay the mighty Caesar, dead.

Silence. The white chill of shock and panic freezing limbs and brains, the senate stood and stared. So fast it had all happened that even those who understood had only risen from their seats, before the final blow was cast.

Cinna was the first to break the spell. 'Liberty! Freedom!' he yelled. 'Tyranny is dead! Run out, proclaim it, cry it about the streets!'

Swiftly Brutus intervened, lest fear should push them out into the streets and turn this triumph to a spreading panic. 'People, senators, be not afraid,' he urged. 'Ambition's debt is paid.' He flung his arms out wide to encompass his fellow conspirators. 'Stoop, Romans, stoop, and let us bathe our hands in Caesar's blood up to the elbows, and besmear our swords: then walk we forth, even to the market-place, and waving our red weapons over our heads, let's all cry, 'Peace, freedom and liberty!'

'Stoop, then, and wash,' cried Cassius exultantly. 'How many ages after this shall this our lofty scene be acted over in states unborn and accents yet unknown! And so often shall we be called the men that gave our country liberty!'

They bent over the bloody shape that lay before them on the ground in tremulous celebration of the sacrifice, each man's head filled with the deed that he had done and the future they believed it bought for them.

Behind them, silent, a new figure entered the senate house, and stood regarding them.

Brutus straightened up, and turned.

It was Mark Antony's servant. He gazed at the bleeding body on the ground. He raised his eyes and spoke to Brutus.

'Thus did my master bid me say,' he said, quietly. 'Brutus is noble, wise, valiant and honest: Caesar was mighty, bold, royal, and loving. Say I love Brutus, and I honour him; say I feared Caesar, honoured and loved him.' Now Antony's servant raised his voice steadily. 'If Brutus will promise that Antony may safely come to him and have explained how Caesar has deserved to lie in death, Mark Antony shall not love Caesar dead as well as Brutus living, but will follow the fortunes and affairs of noble Brutus through the hazards of his untrod state with all true faith. So says my master Antony.'

'Your master is a wise and valiant Roman,' Brutus' voice warmed with relief. 'I never thought him worse. Tell him to come to this place. He shall be satisfied, and, by my honour, depart untouched.' With a nod, the servant left. 'I know that we shall have Antony as a friend,' said Brutus. Would not all true Romans only need to hear their reasons for this deed, to share its triumph, to revel in Rome's new-found liberty?

Cassius shook his head. 'I wish we may have Antony a friend: but yet I have a mind that fears him much . . .'

And Antony was already among them. He entered fast, and seemed to have no eyes for any but the bloody bundle on the ground. He stood in silence over it, his back to them, speaking in low private tones, 'Oh mighty Caesar! Are all your conquests, glories, triumphs shrunk to this little measure?' There was a long silence and impatiently Cassius moved towards him. Brutus caught his arm and motioned him to stay.

Now Mark Antony turned, his face composed and quiet. 'I know not, gentlemen, what you intend, who else must bleed, who else is

rank: if I myself, there is no hour so fit as Caesar's death hour, nor no instrument of half that worth as those your swords, made rich with the most noble blood of all this world. Now, while your purpled hands do reek and smoke, fulfil your pleasure . . .'

'Antony,' interruped Brutus, 'beg not your death of us. Though now we must appear bloody and cruel, our hearts you do not see. They are pitiful; and pity for the general wrong of Rome. To you our swords have leaden points, Mark Antony. Our arms and hearts do receive you in with all kind love, good thoughts and reverence. Only be patient till we have calmed the multitude, beside themselves with fear. And then we will explain the cause, why I, that did love Caesar when I struck him, have done this.'

Antony surveyed them quietly, moving his eyes across each face and bloody hand, though what was in the thoughts passing behind those eyes, no one could tell.

'I do not doubt your wisdom,' he said to them.

'Our reasons are so full of good regard, that were you, Antony, the son of Caesar, you should be satisfied,' Brutus assured him eagerly.

'That's all I seek,' Mark Antony affirmed, 'and ask that I may produce his body in the market-place, and in the pulpit, as a friend, speak at his funeral.'

'You shall, Mark Antony,' cried Brutus, generous in his renewed belief in Antony's goodwill to them.

'Brutus, a word with you,' said Cassius sharply, drawing Brutus to one side. 'You know not what you do,' he hissed. 'Do not consent that Antony speak at his funeral! Do you know how much the people may be moved by that which he will utter?'

Brutus would hear no argument: now that the deed was done, he was exultant in his confidence that all would understand it was a sacrifice for Rome. *He* would speak first in the pulpit and give their reasons, and only after, would Antony address the crowd. The citizens would see that Antony spoke only with Brutus' permission and that the men who had killed Caesar wished him to have all honourable rites and ceremonies in death. Brutus' confidence bounded on: it would appear greatly to their credit to have won the loyalty of Caesar's friend and faithful ally, Mark Antony!

'I like it not,' repeated Cassius doggedly.

But already Brutus was giving these conditions to Mark Antony: he could in his funeral speech speak well of Caesar but may not utter a single word of ill about those who had killed him. And he must make it clear he spoke only by their permission.

'Be it so,' agreed Mark Antony. 'I do desire no more.'

'Prepare the body then, and follow us,' commanded Brutus, and out they went.

Antony was alone. The senate-house had emptied of conspirators and witnesses to their grisly deed. Only the crumpled body of dead Caesar stayed, his blood glistening across the base of Pompey's statue, and Antony, who stood and looked at it.

It was a different Antony from he who spoke soft words of peace to Julius Caesar's killers. He felt the silence drop about the senate halls, and looked up, and on his face was carved a very different tale from that he told to Brutus.

He whispered now, and they were words only for the bleeding corpse before him, 'Oh pardon me, that I am meek and gentle with these butchers! You are the ruins of the noblest man that ever lived in the tide of times.' His voice cracked.

He dropped to his knees beside the body, and in one hand he gripped the shreds of robes, ripped bloody with every dagger's gash into the flesh of Caesar. 'Woe to the hands that shed this costly blood! Over your wounds now do I prophesy, a curse shall light upon the limbs of men; domestic fury and fierce civil strife shall harass all the parts of Italy, and Caesar's spirit, ranging for revenge shall with a monarch's voice cry "Havoc," and let slip the dogs of war!'

In the great central market-place the people waited, grimly restless. Rumours flew from mouth to mouth, half-truths gathered like buzzing bees, grew to monstrous certainties, and then were flung aside. Fear and mourning hung like a shroud about the square.

'We will be satisfied,' the cry went up, and became a chant that swelled and filled the anxious air with ominous mutiny. 'Let us be satisfied. Let us be satisfied.'

Boldly Brutus stepped among them. He raised his hand for silence. At all costs, the vast numbers of people pressing in the square must be divided and then calmed. He urged some to stay and listen to what he had to say, others to go with Cassius and hear his words.

The crowd parted, reformed to shouts and cries, as this or that citizen declared that he would hear Cassius or Brutus. 'And compare

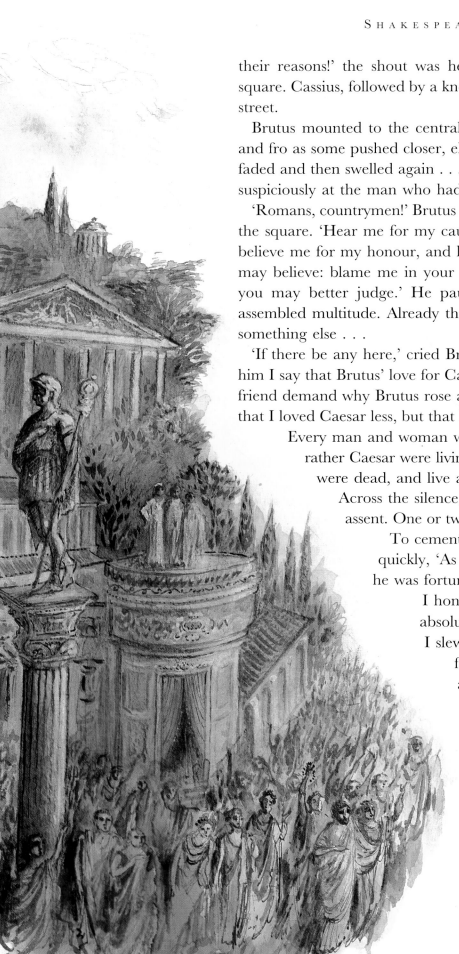

their reasons!' the shout was heard. It hung threatening above the square. Cassius, followed by a knot of yelling men, marched to another street.

Brutus mounted to the central pulpit. Below, the crowd heaved to and fro as some pushed closer, elbowing a path; the noise swelled and faded and then swelled again . . . and, suddenly, silence fell. All stared suspiciously at the man who had, they heard, killed mighty Caesar.

'Romans, countrymen!' Brutus raised his voice and sent it loud across the square. 'Hear me for my cause, and be silent that you may hear: believe me for my honour, and have respect for my honour, that you may believe: blame me in your wisdom, and awake your senses that you may better judge.' He paused and looked slowly around the assembled multitude. Already their sullen curiosity was giving way to something else . . .

'If there be any here,' cried Brutus, 'any dear friend of Caesar's, to him I say that Brutus' love for Caesar was no less than his! If then that friend demand why Brutus rose against Caesar, this is my answer: not that I loved Caesar less, but that I love Rome more!' He paused again. Every man and woman watched. Silence reigned. 'Would you rather Caesar were living, and die all slaves, than that Caesar were dead, and live all free men?'

Across the silence, murmurs rippled: cautious voices of assent. One or two nodded openly: his point was taken.

To cement this hopeful mood, Brutus continued quickly, 'As Caesar loved me, I weep for him; as he was fortunate, I rejoice at it; as he was valiant, I honour him,' again he paused, to ensure absolute attention, 'but as he was *ambitious*, I slew him! There is tears for his love; joy for his fortune; honour for his valour; and *death* for his ambition!'

He leaned across the pulpit, staring hard into the faces of the crowd, 'Who is here so base that he would be a slave? If any, speak, for him have I offended. Who is here that would not be a Roman? If any, speak, for him I have offended.'

Each question rang its insistent rhythm across the square, and as each echo faded, the shaking heads and sympathetic murmurs grew, the rumbling mounting to a single triumphant answer, 'None, Brutus, none!'

Brutus gazed with misting eyes across the mass of Romans spread before him. How clearly, in their nobility, they understood what Brutus and his fellows had to do for liberty in Rome! And would not all right-minded people understand?

A drumbeat boomed across their heads. All turned. Into the square strode Mark Antony, with others, and between them Caesar's body. The murmurs died, stifled by the sight of Julius Caesar's death, so stark and unmistakable.

Sensing the people's shock, Brutus claimed their attention hastily. 'Here comes his body, mourned by Mark Antony: who, though he had no hand in his death, shall receive the benefit of his dying, a place in the commonwealth.' He lifted up his arms, to encompass all of them. '*As which of you shall not?*' He raised a hand again to ask for quiet. 'With this I depart; that, as I slew my best friend for the good of Rome, I shall have the same dagger for myself when it shall please my country to need my death.'

It was as though he had rung a bell to signal ecstasy. The crowd went wild. 'Live, Brutus! live, live!' the nearest cried. And farther off, 'Give him a statue with his ancestors!' And then rising above all else, 'Let him be Caesar!'

Brutus turned his head with sudden shock towards the anonymous cry: a new dictator to replace the old!

Already Mark Antony was mounting the pulpit. He reached the top and surveyed the

crowd. 'For Brutus' sake, I am beholden to you,' he said cautiously.

'It were best he speak no harm of Brutus here!' came a mutter from the crowd.

'This Caesar was a tyrant,' came another. 'We are blest that Rome is rid of him.'

Mark Antony was beginning. 'Friends, Romans, countrymen, lend me your ears.' The murmuring of the crowd fell silent. 'I come to bury Caesar, not to praise him.' Heads nodded, approving this simplicity. To bury was fair; but not to praise a tyrant!

Antony continued, 'The evil that men do lives after them; the good is often interred with their bones: so let it be with Caesar.' He moved to the front edge of the pulpit, and looked down. All stood upon their toes to see. Below him lay the body, gory with its seeping wounds.

'The noble Brutus has told you Caesar was ambitious. If it were so, it was a grievous fault.' He paused again, and continued to gaze upon the corpse. 'And grievously has Caesar answered it.' It was as though the crowd had suddenly become a single watching eye, fastened like a gigantic bird of prey on Antony. 'Here, with the permission of Brutus and the rest, for Brutus is an honourable man . . .' the word lingered in the air, and seemed to pick up echoes, 'so are they all, all *honourable* men . . . I come to speak at Caesar's funeral. He was my friend, faithful and just to me: but Brutus says he was ambitious: and Brutus is an honourable man.'

For a moment it seemed that Antony had finished. Restless movement rippled across the ranks, gloomy with disappointment. But in a moment he began again. And Antony's voice was louder now. 'You all did see that on the feast day I three times presented him a kingly crown, which he three times refused: was this ambition?' More murmurs, quickly dying, lest Antony's next word be lost. 'Yet Brutus says he was ambitious, and sure *he* is an honourable man. I speak not to disprove what Brutus spoke, but here am I to speak what I do know! You did all love him once, not without cause: what cause withholds you then, to mourn for him?' Uneasily, the vast crowd shifted, teetering . . .

And like a cannon's boom, Mark Antony's voice blasted in their ears, 'Oh judgement! You are fled to brutish beasts, and men have lost their reason!' Trembling, he glared across the mass, his face grown white with anger. And then he seemed to shake himself, and spoke more quietly. 'Bear with me: my heart is in the coffin there with Caesar, and I must pause till it come back to me.'

Like a prowling animal now, the crowd writhed, surged a little forward, and from the silence, a muttering . . .

'I think there is much reason in his sayings,' said the citizen who had called Caesar a tyrant. 'Caesar has had great wrong.'

'I fear there will be a worse come in his place,' muttered another man.

'He would not take the crown; therefore it is certain he was not ambitious,' a third concluded.

Antony was speaking again. He surveyed them, measuring, 'Oh masters, if I were disposed to stir your hearts and minds to mutiny and rage, I should do Brutus wrong, and Cassius wrong, who, you all know, are *honourable* men . . .'

He gathered pace, 'Here's a parchment with the seal of Caesar. It is his will. Let but the people hear this testament, and they would go and kiss dead Caesar's wounds and dip their napkins in his sacred blood, beg a hair of him for memory . . .'

'We'll hear the will,' the roar went up, 'read it, Mark Antony. The will! The will! We will hear Caesar's will!'

Antony stood listening to the swelling thunder of the crowd. In all his thinking Brutus had never understood this populace of Rome, this fickle, changing beast, moulded now by Antony into his own brutal weapon of revenge.

'Have patience, gentle friends,' he told them. 'It is not right you know how Caesar loved you. It will inflame you, it will make you mad: it is good you know not that you are his heirs; for if you should, oh, what should come of it!'

'Read the will!' they yelled.

'I fear,' said Antony, 'I wrong the honourable men whose daggers have stabbed Caesar . . .'

'They were traitors: honourable men!' they shrieked.

Antony descended from the pulpit into the crowd and gathered them to Caesar's body to read the will. But first, he lifted up the bloody robes for all to see.

'Look, in this place ran Cassius' dagger through: see what a rent the envious Casca made: through this the well-loved Brutus stabbed. This was the unkindest cut of all; for when the noble Caesar saw him stab, then burst his mighty heart . . . Oh, what a fall was there, my countrymen! Then I, and you, and all of us fell down, whilst bloody *treason* flourished over us.'

The final stone was cast. The multitudes seethed close about the savaged body, like a giant beast that sniffed and whimpered at a fallen friend . . .

And then with one gigantic cry, the fury broke. 'Revenge! Seek! Burn! Fire! Kill! Slay! Let not a traitor live! We'll burn Caesar's body in the holy place, and with the brands fire the traitors' houses!' And from the square they surged, hot with mutiny.

Alone beside the body, Antony breathed deep. Now was Caesar's spirit indeed alive. 'Now let it work. Mischief, you are afoot, take what course you will.' Now would the forces of rivalry for power unlocked by Caesar's death be savagely let loose!

Within twenty-four hours it was Antony, not Brutus, who controlled the city. Brutus and Cassius fled Rome. And into Rome came a powerful ally to Caesar's cause: his young grand-nephew and adopted son and heir, Octavius Caesar.

Rome plunged into bloody chaos, as Antony had prophesied. Citizens raged through the city looking for the murderers of Caesar. In their frenzy to search out their prey even a hapless poet by the name of Cinna, a close friend of Caesar's, was dragged away to death for no other reason than his name: it was the same as Cinna the traitor.

So began a vicious battle for control. In the vacuum left by Julius Caesar's death, Mark Antony, Octavius and a third, named Lepidus, seized power, ruling as triumvirs, dividing all the Roman Empire's territory in Europe, Africa and Asia between themselves. They drew up a list of those to die for treachery against Caesar, coldly bargaining life for life: their own brothers, cousins, nephews, all whom they judged guilty. A hundred senators to die.

In a world torn by the rivalries for power once curbed by Caesar's strength, the power of Antony and Octavius grew unchecked, while Brutus and Cassius, fled separately to exile, prepared for war against them.

At Sardis in Asia Minor, these one-time leaders of the conspiracy met again, each now leading the army legions they had gathered to their cause. Many months had passed since that distant Ides of March in Rome when Caesar fell. The bonds of warmth which tied them then had cooled: in the aftermath of the assassination and their hasty flight, and in this anxious mustering of arms for war, differences once hidden by their common purpose, now reared a menacing head. Each had grown suspicious of the other, and fear of their differences had sown a bitter discord.

How much more than minor quarrels reared their vicious jaws to mangle them! The world whose liberty Brutus had sought by killing Caesar was ripped by bitter quarrels between rival factions, while Octavius and Antony marched on to greater strength. Unwilling to look for the cause of the chaos in the tangled web of their conspiracy, or in illusions of unquestioning honour and righteousness in which he had floated through the deed, Brutus found fault instead with Cassius: Cassius was betraying the nobility of motives for which they had sacrificed Caesar, sullying the honour of their cause with dubious methods for gathering men and money . . .

'Remember March, the Ides of March remember,' he told him angrily. 'Did not great Julius bleed for justice' sake? What villain touched his body, that did stab, and not for justice? What, shall one of us, that struck the foremost man of all this world but for supporting robbers, shall we now contaminate our fingers with base bribes, and sell the mighty space of our large honours for so much trash as may be grasped thus? I had rather be a dog, and bay the moon, than such a Roman!'

'Brutus, bay not me,' warned Cassius, incensed and hurt by Brutus' self-righteous accusations. 'I'll not endure it!'

'There is no terror, Cassius, in your threats,' coldly Brutus rejected Cassius' anger, 'for I am armed so strong in honesty that they pass me as the idle wind . . . I did send to you for certain sums of gold to pay my legions, which you denied me: for I can raise no money by vile means . . .'

'I denied you not,' protested Cassius angrily, 'he was but a fool that brought my answer back!' Fury mixed with a new despair, for suddenly he saw they teetered above a chasm which would split them for evermore. A dark world-weariness swept over him: 'Come, Antony, and young Octavius, come, revenge yourselves alone on Cassius, for Cassius is aweary of the world; hated by one he loves, checked like a slave, all his faults observed, set in a note-book, learned by heart to cast into my teeth!' He rounded sharply on Brutus, 'There is my dagger: strike, as you did at Caesar; for I know, when you did hate him worst, you loved him better than ever you loved Cassius!'

And suddenly they both saw the dark divide that yawned between them, and understood how close they came to plunging into it.

'Sheathe your dagger,' said Brutus quietly. Wearily he hauled at

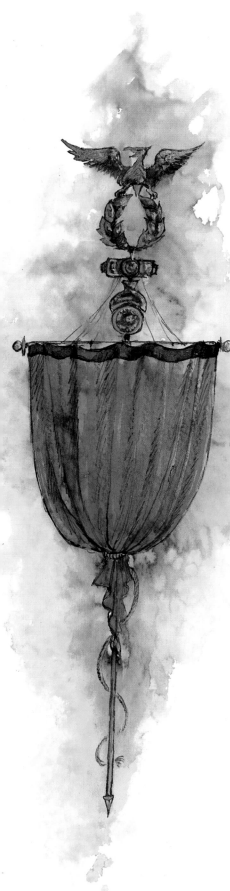

their years of trusted friendship to patch up their differences. At their peril they had ignored them when they planned the death of Caesar.

And Brutus was sicker at heart than Cassius could have guessed. He had just heard that his beloved wife, plunged deep in grief at his exile and the growing strength of Octavius with Mark Antony, had killed herself. He turned again toward his faith in Cassius and that vision of Rome's freedom which had spurred him on to what he'd done. What else was there to grasp at, as the war with Octavius and Mark Antony drew nearer? Already these two had reached Philippi in Greece.

Brutus was all for marching straight to fight. Cassius thought differently: better to exhaust the enemy with marching, while they, merely awaiting their arrival, would be well-prepared.

Brutus disagreed. It was with the same confidence that he had rejected killing Mark Antony and insisted on him speaking in the market-place at Caesar's funeral. If they allowed the enemy to march from Philippi, he argued, the enemy would gather people to their ranks in every land they passed through . . .

'Hear me, good brother,' protested Cassius desperately.

'Our legions are brimful, our cause is ripe,' insisted Brutus. 'The enemy increases every day. We, at the height, are ready to decline. There is a tide in the affairs of men, which, taken at the flood, leads on to fortune: omitted, all the voyage of their life is bound in shallows and in miseries. On such a full sea are we now afloat, and we must take the current when it serves, or lose our ventures.'

As before, Cassius gave in. 'Then, with your will, go on; we'll along ourselves, and meet them at Philippi.' There was no more to say.

In his tent, Brutus sought a kind of peace, listening to the strains of music played by a sleepy servant. He read awhile, or tried to, searching the words that clustered on the page for some hint of certainty in the grim time that loomed ahead, until the room grew strangely dark, and struggling to clear his aching eyes, he suddenly froze. A dark chill had crept into the tent, making the flickering candle gutter, and a shadow moved across the gloom, formless, growing stronger, swelling grotesquely into the shape of murdered Caesar.

'Why do you come?' breathed Brutus, shivering.

'To tell you that you shall see me at Philippi,' echoed the sombre voice of Caesar's ghost.

At Philippi the rival armies met: Cassius and Brutus facing young Octavius Caesar and Mark Antony.

'Words before blows: is it so, countrymen?' challenged Brutus.

'Not that we love words better, as you do,' retorted Octavius.

'Good words are better than bad strokes, Octavius,' Brutus replied.

'In your bad strokes, Brutus, you give good words,' said Antony. 'Witness the hole you made in Caesar's heart, crying "Long live! hail, Caesar!" Villains! You showed your teeth like apes, and fawned like hounds, and bowed like slaves, kissing Caesar's feet; whilst damned Casca, like a cur, behind struck Caesar in the neck!'

Octavius became impatient: hot words bandied were no alternative to the cold logic of brandished steel. 'Look,' he cried, 'I draw a sword against conspirators! When think you that the sword goes up again? Never, till Caesar's three and thirty wounds be well avenged; or till another Caesar has added slaughter to the sword of traitors!'

Compelled against his judgement to risk everything in this single battle here at Philippi, Cassius faltered before a sense of gathering doom. 'If we lose this battle,' he said to Brutus, 'then is this the very last time we shall speak together.'

Brutus looked long and hard into his friend's face, a forgotten gentleness between them warming the coldness of the future he too sensed. 'This same day must end that work the Ides of March began,' he murmured, 'and whether we shall meet again I know not.' He clasped Cassius' hand. 'Therefore our everlasting farewell take: for ever, and for ever, farewell, Cassius! If we do meet again, why, we shall smile. If not, why then, this parting was well made! Oh that a man might know the end of this day's business before it comes!'

That day did end the work the Ides of March began. On one flank Brutus pushed forward an attack on Octavius' force, and won. But he gave the signal to attack too early for Cassius' legions: forced into battle ill-prepared, they were swiftly overrun by Antony's troops.

Sinking ever deeper in despair, Cassius misread the signs of victory on Brutus' flank: watching his soldiers greeted eagerly by their victorious fellows, he thought that he had seen his troops vanquished by the enemy.

This was Cassius' day of birth: on this day he had entered the world, and suddenly he knew it was the day that he would leave it. Bowing before the overwhelming misery of the defeat he believed had overtaken them, he chose the traditional fate of Romans in defeat: death by his own hand. He gave his servant one final task: to guide the same sword that killed Julius Caesar into Cassius' breast.

Brutus, flushed with the excitement of his early victory against Octavius' force, received the news of Cassius' death like the knell of doom. He rushed to the body of his friend. Now that same despair which had taken Cassius dropped like a shroud over Brutus. 'Oh Julius Caesar, you are mighty yet!' he cried. 'Your spirit walks abroad, and turns our swords into our own entrails! The last of all the Romans, fare well!' he mourned. 'Friends, I owe more tears to this dead man than you shall see me pay. I shall find time, Cassius,' he whispered, 'I shall find time.'

Before the day was out, Brutus tried their fortunes in a second fight. This time there was no victory: as the light of that ill-chosen day began to fade, the remnants of his defeated force clung with him and sought sanctuary in the creeping dark of night. And Brutus, who had sworn to Cassius that in defeat he would not look for death, now saw only this escape ahead of him.

'The ghost of Caesar has appeared to me two separate times by night: at Sardis once, and, this last night, here in Philippi fields: I know my hour is come,' he whispered.

'Not so, my lord,' his companions argued.

'I am sure it is,' he said again. 'Our enemies have beat us to the pit: it is more worthy to leap in ourselves, than wait until they push us. I shall have more glory by this losing day than Octavius and Mark Antony by this vile conquest shall attain,' he vowed and rallied his remaining strength of purpose, 'Brutus' tongue has almost ended his life's history: night hangs upon my eyes: my bones would rest, that have but laboured to attain this hour . . .'

And as he ran upon the sword held by his faithful servant, he gasped to the man whose death had haunted him each minute since that fateful Ides of March, 'Caesar, now be still,' and died.

Victorious Antony came upon the body of his enemy, and stood looking down at it. It was the final pinnacle of his success; and yet the taste of it was, in this moment, bitter.

'This was the noblest Roman of them all,' he mourned. 'All the conspirators, save only he, did what they did in envy of great Caesar; he only, in general honest thought and common good to all, made one of them. His life was gentle, and the elements so mixed in him that Nature might stand up and say to all the world, "This was a man!"'

Octavius stood by his side. Now was the murder of Julius Caesar finally revenged; ahead lay only the fruits of victory. There was no power in the Roman world could challenge the might of Octavius and Mark Antony combined. For the moment, at least, they stood together.